YEAR OF THE

F
O
O
L

by

John Kreilkamp

Copyright © 2016 John Kreilkamp

All rights reserved.

Cover design by Michelle Rene Goodhew of Mundus Media Ink
http://MundusMediaInk.com

"My story is not a pleasant one, it is neither sweet nor harmonious, ... it has the taste of nonsense and chaos, of madness and dreams..."

Hermann Hesse from DEMIAN

John Kreilkamp

PART ONE

SEEKING

Chapter 1

Suddenly, it was over, I was awake. As mysteriously as the experience had started, it ended. I sat up in bed, turned on a lamp and looked around. Yes, everything looked familiar, everything was how it should be. Whatever it was, it was now gone. It was just me here now, same as usual. It was still a hot humid summer night in Washington, D. C.

I breathed a big sigh of relief. I was shaking. It felt so nice to be feeling my normal self again. I got up and moved around, trying to clear my head, but my mind kept going back to the presence I had just felt in my room.

Then a loud explosion, another ... another ... a truck backfiring on Wisconsin Avenue? My mind was spinning, looking for a reasonable explanation. Or was there a connection between that loud sound and my own inner state? Ridiculous! How could those sounds have anything to do with what had just happened to me?

But then, what had just happened to me? I grabbed the pen and notebook by my bed and started writing.

In the morning I went through my usual routine of looking through the newspaper for rooms to rent. For several months now I had been trying to move out of my parents' house where I'd been living for the past year. I knew I needed to be on my own, but I had found nothing that suited my purposes.

The problem was that I wanted to live cheaply so I could continue spending most of my time studying piano and music. Most of my friends were living communally, renting houses together. I knew from hanging out with them that I would get nothing done in that kind of situation, too many distractions. I needed privacy.

That morning there was a promising ad in the paper, and I called the number and made an appointment to meet the couple that evening. When I got there I learned the couple was a middle-aged woman, Jane, and her teenage daughter, Melissa, who was out somewhere. Jane invited me in and led me to the living room, which I was happy to see had a piano in it, and we sat on the couch.

Jane was attractive, with beautiful eyes and a very serious expression. She started with the obvious question. "What do you do? Tell me something about yourself."

Oddly enough, when I had checked into other rentals, no one had sat down with me on the couch to ask me about myself. Everyone had been aloof and professional - here's the room, here are the rules. So, this was a welcome change.

"I want to write music. so I have been studying piano and music theory and that's mainly how I want to spend my time. I have some money saved and so I want to focus on writing music."

"What kind of music do you want to write?"

"I don't know how to describe it." I hesitated, gathering my thoughts.

She wasted no time and pointing at the piano, said, "Play me something you've written."

I was extremely shy about playing in public for strangers, had a real hang-up about it, but I knew this was something I had to be able to do. So, I muttered some lame excuses about the piece I was about to play and then I went to the piano and played it, not very inspired, but I got through it. It's a weird little piece of music. No real tune in it, and a strange mixed up beat, doesn't really go anywhere.

When I finished I looked at Jane and said, "That's it." I felt embarrassed.

"That's ... like you say, difficult to describe. But I liked it! Can I ask you, why aren't you going to a music school?"

I quickly got myself off the piano bench and back safely on the couch. "Yeah, good question. I was a music major at the University of Oregon, but I didn't like it, it felt too much like training to become a music teacher, which I don't want to do. And I have been studying with a really good piano teacher here, who has also been teaching me about composition."

My piano teacher was also a well-known composer, at least in the D.C. area, and he wrote the prototypical modern classical music, pretty much impossible to listen to with no recognizable melody or harmonies. His style had definitely influenced me in the piano piece I had played for her.

And, I did not add that I had, in fact, just stopped lessons because I felt I had gone as far as I needed to go with him. After a year of intense practicing, I could now play the piano well enough to compose music. Since I was not interested in becoming a concert pianist, I didn't see the point in more lessons. And also, I didn't want to write music like the music he wrote.

So, then we got onto the subject of how I had ended up so far away at the university of Oregon, and as we continued to talk, I was starting to feel very comfortable sitting there talking to her. I was thinking that this could be it, exactly what I was looking for.

She then said something which was to later prove prophetic. "Your eyes really lit up when I asked you about Oregon. Do you miss being out there?"

I nodded my head somewhat ambiguously as I didn't know what to say. I had not really thought about Oregon in a while. Her saying that though about my eyes lighting up made me suddenly realize that, of course, I *did* miss Oregon. It was such a carefree life out there compared to D. C. I had been so focused on learning the piano that I had not even allowed myself to think about how much I missed it. I had been on a mission, and I could not afford to sit around thinking about how much fun I could be having if I was still living in Eugene.

I said lamely, "Yeah, it was fun being out there, but I am here now."

She then explained that she and her daughter were out most of the day and I would be free to play the piano as much as I wanted. I felt for sure she would want me to live there, since we seemed to be getting along.

She then asked me what kind of books I liked, and I told her the books I was currently reading, mainly about psychology, a book about Gestalt Therapy by Fritz Perls, and Jung's book, *Memories, Dreams, Reflections.* I also mentioned *In Search of the Miraculous,* a book about the author, Ouspensky, on a spiritual quest and his meeting with the mysterious teacher, G. I'd been reading it off and on for a couple years and had recently picked it up again. It was one of those books that I had never been able to finish. The material was too rich, deep, dense. I would read a page or two and have to put it down to try and understand it.

Her eyes widened, "John, I know that book very well. Tell me what you like about it."

"Well, what G says is amazing. What he says about human beings are asleep, and that they need to remember themselves. Which I don't understand, but something about it sounds right. What does it mean to you, self-remembering?"

So far she had been the one asking questions, so, I felt good about being able to finally ask her something.

She sat back on the couch and stared at the ceiling. I was enjoying this experience of having an intelligent conversation with her, that she happened to be an attractive older female certainly added an unusual element to the mix. And, just as importantly, we were talking about Ouspensky's book. A friend in Oregon had turned me on to this book, but none of my friends in D.C. were into this kind of thing. In fact, this was another thing I missed about Eugene, my friends were different there than the ones I had in D. C.

Finally, she said, "I don't think I can tell you much. Other than it's something that you need to work on. It's called work. Working on yourself."

"Yeah, that phrase is in that book, working on yourself. But how do you do it? I mean, what do you do?"

"It's something you do in the moment. But, John, I know you really want to know, and I feel bad about this answer I am giving you. But, I would, basically, have to tell you everything I know, in order to answer your question about self-remembering. In other words it can't be answered in a sentence or two sitting on the couch like this."

I understood what she was saying, but my thought was, well, can't you at least throw me a crumb?

She went on, "I have a question for you though, how do *you* plan to search for the miraculous?"

The question caught me off guard. Oddly enough, even though I was really intrigued by the book, I had never asked myself that question before. And then I remembered the dream experience I'd had the night before and I blurted out, "Just last night, I had a really strange experience. It was like a dream, but it was really feeling a presence in the room with me."

And then I hesitated. Was it really smart to talk about this with her since I want to rent a room from her? First, that ridiculous piano piece, and now I'm telling her this crazy dream I had?!

"Go on!" She said. "Why are you stopping?"

"I don't know, it's so weird, really. Anyway, so, I woke up in the middle of the night and I felt a presence in the room with me, and I was *so* terrified by feeling this presence, that I could not enjoy what happened. A bunch of stuff happened, and I won't tell you all of it, but, like, there was this beautiful sound, of feet shuffling on a marble floor, and girls voices in the air, echoing, like we were in a giant dome. And then at some point I felt a breeze coming through the open windows in my bedroom blowing on the back of my head, and the wind got stronger and stronger until it was actually parting my hair in back. And then it became a hand on the back of my neck, massaging the back of my neck. And again, my terror became even stronger. And all my efforts went into trying to wake up, or trying to move, because I felt like I was under some kind of spell, and all I needed to do to break this spell was move. But I couldn't move. Anyway, at some point, quite suddenly, it was over. And I felt normal. There was no more presence in the room."

"Wow! What do you think it means?"

"Uh, I have no idea! But when you asked me, about how I plan to search for the miraculous, I thought of this dream. I mean, the miraculous did happen last night, at least as far as I am concerned. But I have no idea what to do about it."

"John, thank you so much for telling me about that. So interesting. Ya know, I want to read you a letter I got today." And she left the room.

When she returned, she was holding a few pages in her hand. "This letter is from a friend in California, her name is Caroline. She is also in the work."

She read the letter. In it Caroline described her difficulties in overcoming certain tendencies in her personality. and she quoted some writer I was not familiar with. I found it fascinating, she was describing some situation she was living in, and the letter was clearly meant to inspire the reader into being serious about the work.

When Jane finished reading it, I felt something momentous was taking place. But I had no idea what to do, or if I was supposed to do anything. The moment felt momentous - what a funny word - because I was hearing first-hand and directly from people who were "working on themselves." I was not just reading about it in a book.

Jane said, "When you told me your dream I thought of Caroline. She is psychic, even though she did not mention anything about that in her letter. She has had experiences similar to the one you described to me. And she is a very, very inspiring friend for me."

"So, how do I learn more? Are you in an organization or a group of some kind?"

She hesitated and then said slowly, "I am not in an organization, but this is not something I can talk about with you now. And I know I am coming across as secretive, but, please understand, we need to go slowly with this subject. I can tell you this though, people in the work naturally find other people in the work. Just like you have found me. Seems like we have met purely by chance, but was it? Once you're in the work, everything has a meaning, and there are no chance meetings. Well, I should say there is the possibility for that. You have now met me, I think this is enough for now."

We went over a few details about the rent. she wanted me to come and have dinner with her and her daughter. I was supposed to call her in a few days to set up an evening for that.

As she was leading me to the front door, her daughter came home.

Jane said, "Melissa, you came back just in time. This is John, he is looking for a room to rent, and he might be living with us."

We said hello to each other, and I noticed that Melissa seemed to be extremely upset about something, like she had been crying.

Jane said, "Melissa, tell John about the meetings you go to." Melissa looked flustered and gave a big sigh. "I'm sure he is interested. Melissa is a premie, do you know about premies, John? They talk about love, love for ..."

Suddenly, Melissa burst into tears and shouted at her mother to stop and then she ran out of the room and I could hear her running up the stairs.

Jane and I looked at each other, and Jane said, "I am sorry, she is not usually like this. I don't know what that's about."

Something about this struck me as unfortunate, and I hoped it would not hurt my chances of living there.

"I have never heard of premies."

"Premies believe in love, it's all about love for their guru. He's just a teenager. you've probably read about him in the paper."

I tried to lighten the mood and said, "Funny, when I was fifteen, all the girls were in love with the Beatles. Now, it's a guru!"

We said our good-byes, and as I went home, I was feeling very good, certain that I had finally found a suitable place to live.

A few days passed and I called Jane. She told me there had been a change in plans. Her sister needed a place to stay and so she would be staying with them and so she no longer had a room to rent. She apologized and wished me well, and that was that. I suspected it was really because her daughter had burst into tears in front of me; however, there was nothing I could do about that, and reality set in. I still had not found a place to live, time was passing, and nothing could really start happening for me as long as I was living under my parents' watchful eyes. I had to be on my own, but it was too expensive in the big city of Washington D. C.

I had several more occurrences of the nighttime presence. One night was particularly intriguing. I saw a blackboard with formulas on it, and endless symbols and numbers were floating in the air all around me. But, I could not enjoy the sight because of the fear which gripped my body. I could not sit back and see what it was showing me, all my efforts went into trying to shake out of the physical paralysis my fear created.

Once the presence was gone, and I was back in my normal consciousness, I instinctively took my pen and notebook and started to write out a description of what had happened.

And then I nearly jumped out of bed.

It was Jane's voice ringing in my ears, asking me the question: How do you plan to search for the miraculous?

And the answer was suddenly so obvious! I realized the question was not *how,* but *when*? And the answer was obviously *now*! I needed to search for the miraculous! And I didn't need to figure out how to do it, I just needed to start. It was not enough to read a book about someone else searching for the miraculous, I needed to do what Ouspensky had done.

When Jane had asked me, I had blown off that question as something impossible to answer, but now, I realized, that was the *most* important question for me. And the dream experiences were just making it even more urgent that I get going on my search.

A cloud was lifting, I was seeing my immediate future in front of me. I needed to find out what was happening inside me that was producing these experiences, and, just as importantly, what was in the way of my being able to just enjoy them. Along with this realization came the thought that I needed to get serious about learning how to meditate, how to control my thoughts, how to control my mind. I felt there was a connection between these experiences and my uncontrollable thinking since during these experiences I could not control the fear. I figured that if I could control my mind, I would not be so susceptible to this overwhelming fear.

And even more importantly, I realized this was more important than my obsessive study of music and piano. In the past year I'd become much better at the piano. I was now able to play complex and challenging pieces that a year before would have been out of the question. Diabolically, the better I got, the more worried I became. Why? Because I was terrified about having to one day do something with my growing ability - namely, for people to listen to me perform at the piano.

One day at home I played, flawlessly, a piece by Beethoven, and my father came into the study with a big, beaming smile on his face and said, "John, that was perfect, that will be one of the pieces you will play at your first concert!"

I looked at him in shock. He was actually thinking about my first concert!

But, whenever I mentioned cautiously to friends and family my fear of performing, it was pooh-poohed as something everyone went through. I had an older brother in theater who confided to me that after years of performing on the stage he often threw up from nervousness before the show. That did not make me feel any better.

All of this was a factor in my "quest". Yes, I wanted to find an answer to what was coming to me in these wild nighttime visions. An answer to why I was so terrified of that unseen presence in the room. And I also understood I needed to grow in a more practical way. What good was any musical skill I gained if I was afraid to play? I needed to lose my fears - not only my fear of being in the room with an unseen presence, but my fear of being in the room with seen presences, human beings.

So, what had been such a problem for me the last few months, how to get out on my own, was suddenly not a problem anymore. I knew what I needed to do next. It was not study music more, I'd already learned enough about the piano and music to start composing. What I needed to do was take care of my inner state. And as far as a plan goes, I didn't even really have to think about making a plan, it was obvious to me that the first step was to go back out to Oregon. Cheaper rentals, the college town atmosphere, my friends there, and Jane's comment that my eyes lit up when i was talking about Oregon.

The next night I was hanging out with my old friends Daryl and Ray. Daryl was living with his older sister and her boy friend in a cool old house. I would have been welcomed to live there, but this was the kind of scene that I knew would be a disaster since all Daryl did was take drugs.

I was telling them about my idea to go back out to Oregon. They were both incredulous, could not believe that I was planning yet another trip out west. I had already dropped out twice from college and so this would be my third trip back out to Oregon. What had been so clear to me the night before was impossible to explain to them.

Ray got up on his high horse and proclaimed, "So, you want to make another trip to the promised land, eh? When are you going to figure out that what you are looking for is not out west in Oregon, and it's not back east either. You need to settle down and apply yourself to something. And you too, Daryl! Decide what you want to study and go back to school, that's what you should be doing, not chasing some ridiculous idea about the meaning of life."

Daryl's sister Daria wandered in and wanted us to join them downstairs for a smoke. Joe, her boyfriend, had just scored some hash.

I'd had a crush on Daria for years. She was older than her brother and tall and shapely, but she was going with Joe, a much older guy who claimed to have hung out with the Beats in the 50's. But Joe claimed a lot of things, and I was pretty skeptical of everything he said.

Soon we were all getting high sitting around their dining room table. I told them I was considering going back out to Oregon and tried to tell them about the experiences I'd been having.

Daryl said, "Hey, that sounds like a flashback or something."

"But I never felt a presence when tripping! So, how could it be a flashback?"

"Look, John, a flashback does not have to be literally, repeating an experience you had on acid. It is more a similar type of experience."

"But, okay, so what if it *is* a flashback? How does that really explain anything? I mean, it's still this really strange thing happening to me!"

Ray said, "John, let me ask you, why aren't you going to an expert in the field? Like, maybe, a psychiatrist? They are trained to help people who are having experiences like this. What is traveling to the promised land going to do for you? You're having some strange psychological shit happening. They have experience with understanding weird stuff, you should talk to someone who knows about the mind."

"Ray, do you really think any doctor is going to have a clue about this kind of thing?"

"Well, I don't know, but maybe, I mean there's always the chance."

I had no response to that. I did not see these mysterious episodes as part of my psychological makeup. And even if they were, I had no faith that a psychiatrist would have a clue as to what should be done about them.

Joe had a deck of cards he kept shuffling and moving around. I could see it was that Tarot deck he always had with him. I knew really nothing about it, other than I was intrigued by the cards' images. *The Hanged Man* struck me as especially significant.

I asked, "Who made up the Tarot deck?"

Joe shrugged his shoulders.

Daria said, "Joe, do a reading on John, see if he should go to Oregon or not."

Joe looked at me, "It's your call, man. I'll do a reading but only if you request it. These cards are some serious shit, man."

Daria said, "Joe is amazing at reading these cards, you have to do it, John, please."

Since it was Daria asking me to do it, I knew I had no choice.

I said, "Okay, so, what do I do?"

Joe said, "What do you do? Nothing! I'm the one who does the reading for you. You just sit back and try to stay calm. So, the question is …?"

"Oh, yeah, well, about going to Oregon. Will I find what I am looking for out in Oregon? Is that a good question?"

He shrugged his shoulders. "I don't know, man, it's your question."

I thought some more. "How about, should I go to Oregon?"

He held the deck out to me and said, "Just hold it for a moment."

I took it and held it for a moment and then handed it back.

Joe took a breath, smiled an evil grin and pulled out a card and put it on the table in front of me. I looked at it. It was the Fool. Joe nodded his head slowly. Daria laughed. Daryl and Ray laughed.

I looked at the card more closely and could see it showed a guy walking along enjoying the beautiful day, but he was about to walk off a cliff.

"So, what does this mean? That I should not go?"

Joe said, "To tell you the truth, man ... I have no idea!"

This really made Daryl crack up. When he started laughing, especially when he was stoned, he could not stop. All he could say was, "It's so perfect!"

Joe said, "It's just one card, there's more to come. But that card there, that's your card. That is you! That represents you."

And everyone kept laughing.

Daria stood up and staggered over and wrapped her arms around me. "Oh, John, that is such a perfect card for you, really! It's a beautiful card, it's like one of my favorite cards, really, one of my very favorite cards." She sighed. "The Fool!

Joe said, "Okay, okay, let's quit the fooling around, Daria, we're in the middle of a reading. So, tell me, when is your birthday? And what year?"

I told him. He was computing something, then he smiled. "Hey, you really are the Fool! Your numbers add up to twenty two, that's the number of the Fool!"

Daria said, "Wow, that's amazing!"

This got Daryl excited. "Hey, how do you figure that out?"

Joe ignored him. "So, we have established that you are definitely the Fool, so let's get on with the rest of the reading."

He drew another card and put it right on top of the first card. It was the Hanged Man. Daryl gasped. The room was suddenly quiet, no more laughing.

Joe broke the spell by saying, "You know what, man, I don't need to draw any more cards. That says it all. Those two cards give you the answer."

I looked at him, waiting. He was a great one for drawing out the drama. He slowly lit a cigarette. "The Hanged Man crosses you. That means it's your obstacle, what you should avoid. Now, what does the Hanged Man mean? It means being stuck, doing nothing, not taking any action. So, that means you definitely should go, you should take action, to go against the Hanged Man."

I followed that. "But what about the Fool? What does that mean?"

"Hey, nothing you can do about that, it's your destiny. You put yourself at the mercy of the world, so yeah, go out to Oregon. In a way, nothing can harm the Fool, so don't worry about it. If it's what you feel like doing, you should do it. It's the perfect thing for the Fool to do! And you know what, even better, is that you will turn twenty-two on your next birthday. So, go forth, young man, be the Fool!"

So, it was full steam ahead! I found a guy driving all the way to Reed College in Oregon who needed help with driving. This was a stroke of luck that would put me just a few hours from Eugene. However, we had a major disagreement just west of Chicago. I wanted us to stop and sleep, and he wanted us to take speed so we could drive on, drive all the way without even stopping to rest. I said no way. I'd had experience with speed and knew it was not something I ever wanted to take again. So, he let me out in a small town in western Illinois where I bought a bus ticket to take me the rest of the way.

As I sat there waiting in this small town, I realized how glad I was to be alone. I wanted to savor the journey across the country, not drive through it in a meth haze. The great Plains - the flat lands of Illinois, Iowa, Nebraska - are considered boring to traverse, but I found them mesmerizing when I was actually there, smack dab in the middle of it all. I sat back and relaxed, grateful to not have to make conversation with anyone. I could look out the window and let my mind wander.

As the bus made its way across the barren landscapes of Wyoming and Utah and then into the picture postcard valleys of Idaho, something in me relaxed. I had done it, I was now out west, once again I had gotten myself out of the crowded, busy, frenetic eastern half of the country.

I felt giddy, excited, relieved. I smiled thinking about Ray's idea that I was merely putting off making a decision about my future. If I was putting it off, so what? The longer I can put it off, the better off I was!

Beauty is a wonderful antidote to the weighty matters of life. Witnessing the earth outside the bus window stretching off into the distance was soothing and exciting at the same time. I patted myself on the shoulder and congratulated myself. "Yes, John, old boy, you have done it again, now this is an America to be proud of, this is America the Beautiful!"

The bus gradually emptied itself of its passengers until I was alone with two other people about my age, a guy and a girl, and at some point we started talking. I noticed an unusually shaped book they had, and I asked them about it. The girl handed it to me; it had the title, *Be Here Now,* and the author was an Indian named Ram Dass. She said a guy they had met had given it to them, and they had been reading it for the last week.

"So, who is Ram Dass?"

"He's an American who got his name from a guru."

That made me skeptical. "Well, what's it about?"

The girl excitedly told me, "Oh, it is amazing. You know Timothy Leary, well, the guy who wrote this book used to teach at Harvard with Leary and then he dropped acid, got fired, and went to India to look for truth."

Then the guy laughed and said, "Oh man, did he ever find it! This is really… " he patted the book, "it's the real thing, man. You gotta get yourself turned on to it, man."

I was struck by the phrase "look for truth." And I turned myself around and looked skeptically at *my* skeptical state of mind. Maybe this book was *exactly* what I needed to read.

The girl started reading some of it out loud. I became spellbound by what I was hearing. When it was time for them to disembark the girl told me that the guy who had given them the book had told them when they finished it, they should give it away to someone deserving. And so, she made me promise that when I finished it I would also give it away.

I agreed, and so she handed me the book. I read it off and on until the bus got to Eugene. It was amazing. Its basic message was - still is of course - that if one could live in the present moment, and *only* in the present moment, one would truly be alive and enlightened. Simple or not, obvious or not, it hit my 21-year-old brain like a ton of bricks. Of course nothing exists that is not in this moment; all else is either our memories about what happened in the past or our plans for what will happen in the future - but none of that actually *exists*. Life is in this moment, there is nothing more to it.

It reminded me of a reaction I'd had to another popular expression of my generation. When I was living in a dorm as a freshman, some girls put up a huge sign outside their dorm window that read, *Today is the first day of the rest of your life.* When I first saw that sign, I was filled with an incredible feeling of hope and optimism. I thought, what an amazing way to look at today! Of course after the sign had been up for several weeks, the initial impact the words had made on me was long gone, and the expression has since become a cynical joke.

And now again I had that surge of optimism and hope. Life is simple, there is only this moment. And all I have to do is to live *now*, in *this moment.* And how difficult can that be? It just means being here, now. Right here, now. And now. And now. Moments later, I realized I had been far away from the present moment. I was thinking of what my father would say about this simplistic message. He was a philosophy professor and tended to be a snob about certain new ideas, but then sometimes he was also open-minded and would see them as extensions of Socrates' teaching. And wham, just like that, imagining an imaginary conversation with my father, I was somewhere other than here now, and for who knows how long.

The book's other message, or at least what I got out of it, was that the author had been traveling in India and had found a teacher, a guru, who had enlightened him. His mind had been opened up, specifically his third eye, and that was how he had been able to write this book

I had heard about the existence of a third eye, but I'd never met anyone who could tell me what it was or how to see through it or whether I had one or how I could get one, or how to access it. I was not a believer or non-believer in the third eye, but I did have curiosity about it, so maybe that did make me a believer.

As far as the idea of a guru, I had read *Autobiography of a Yogi* and that was all about a guru with incredible powers. I had friends who refused to believe it, but I had no problem accepting that some people could develop powers beyond what most people have. I was open to believing that this writer of the book *Be Here Now* was telling the truth, that he had met someone who had the ability to help him. But still I had no desire to travel to India and search for a guru. Something seemed off about that. And most importantly, I felt very good about being on my way to Oregon, and I was excited to see what would happen next.

Chapter 2

When I arrived in Eugene I had no definite place to stay although I knew I could probably crash with various old friends. As a way of celebrating my return, I immediately went to what had been my favorite hang-out, the Odyssey Café. I figured I'd probably run into someone I knew, and sure enough, outside the café on the street, my old roommate Alonzo was standing like an egret.

When I'd been a student, I had lived with Alonzo one year and for a time we were almost inseparable. He was 6'7", black and from the south side of Chicago, and epitomized the new age spiritual seeker who saw profound truths everywhere and made a point of sharing them with anyone and everyone. He was also *always* practicing something, disciplining himself, and in this moment it was ballet, hence his egret stance, left foot resting on the right knee while he tried to maintain a still pose.

Alonzo was a wild card, way out of the main stream. As close as we had been, we'd also clashed. We were both born under the sign of Aquarius and maybe we were too much alike; we had the classic hot/cold friendship. But all that was forgotten. He was overjoyed to see me and let out a loud whoop and grabbed me in a big hug.

"John, you're here! This is great! What a surprise! I didn't know for sure if I'd ever see you again."

His smiling dark face made my heart glad. "It's good to see you again Alonzo. I just arrived in town and you are the first person I see! I think that's a very good sign!"

"Where have you been?"

"I've been on the east coast, back home in Washington D.C."

"And now you're out here? I mean, to stay?"

"Yeah, I just arrived, I mean, literally just arrived. About thirty minutes ago. On the bus. As you can see." I pointed to the big duffel bag I had carried my stuff across the country in.

"Wow, this is amazing. You come to the Odyssey Café and you run into your old best buddy, Alonzo, and Alonzo is happy to see you! Where are you staying?"

"Good question. I don't know, I don't have a place to stay tonight. Do you have room?"

"I do! Sure I do, I have plenty of room. Hey, we need to talk, I can feel that what's happening with you is important. I've got some dynamite weed and we can smoke and listen to music and play music and talk and smoke some more."

At some point during the night, I told him about my nighttime dreams and visions of an unseen presence. He became quite animated.

"John, I am so happy for you. I knew you had something like this coming. Something is contacting you. I knew you were destined for something."

"Yes, that's right, something is contacting me, that's how it feels, but why the hell can't I relax and enjoy the contact?"

"I don't know, but at least you recognize that you aren't relaxed and you want to be. Now you have to discover what will relax you. Hey, is *this* why you came back to Eugene, to find out?"

I nodded my head. I was feeling very fine about being in Eugene again. It felt like I was on the right track. I didn't know where this track would lead but knew there was something out there waiting to be discovered, like I had found the secret again, the feeling of life being an outrageous journey, a journey on which anything can happen.

"That's fantastic! That's the most important thing, you have a feeling that *here,* in Eugene, is where you should be! Then I am sure you will find it. And you know what? You have changed, I can tell. Remember how I used to get so frustrated with you, trying to get you to feel the love all around you, his love, you know, the Lord's love?"

He started smiling his goofy smile again. Just mentioning the Lord's love put Alonzo into a strange dreamy state.

"Yes, of course I remember. But that's …"

"No, wait, don't argue with me, this is not something to argue about. Just listen to your old friend, Alonzo. I know. I know, John. This is not about me against you, my ego fighting against your ego. I'm telling you, *you* now know."

I laughed nervously. "Okay, seriously, Alonzo, tell me what you think I now know. I don't think I know, I mean I know that I don't know what you are talking about. I don't feel this is a thing about God or the Lord. Something is contacting me, and it's far out, but I don't think of it as God, or like a religious experience. I mean, not at all."

Frustrated he stared into my eyes. "John, are you really making me spell it out for you? Okay, fine, I can play along."

He took a nice long hit off the joint, held it a long, long moment, and then let it out slowly.

"Okay, well, let's just say that now you know there's something *greater* than you."

I thought about that and realized that yes, I could accept that, and Alonzo was right, and it was stupid for me to have argued the point. I had changed, I had been contacted and I was now actively seeking guidance. I had been hooked into something and it was leading me along, and I was following my impulses which I had the feeling were coming from the contact I'd had with the unexplainable nighttime experiences.

I remembered the disagreements, the major arguments we'd had when we lived together in the small cottage behind the Women's Club of Eugene. Alonzo's favorite song was "Amazing Grace" and he was so disappointed I did not share his enthusiasm for that song, and in fact I flat out did not like the song. I blamed it all on my Catholic upbringing. I didn't like the song because I had been brainwashed to believe in the "one true religion." I didn't want to hear anymore about grace saving a wretch like me. I had been raised in a repressed Catholic family, and I disliked anything that reminded me of that.

That made no sense to Alonzo because he said this is not about religion, this is about a feeling for the Lord, for the mysterious presence behind everything.

I could never explain or maybe I could never admit to Alonzo the real reason I didn't like the song, which was because it made me realize that I didn't know what grace was. I had not had the experience of feeling grace. I knew Alonzo was not faking his depth of feeling for the song, and I knew I did not have that depth.

I didn't want to get into all that again, and I did not see any reason to explain that I *still* did not want to sing "Amazing Grace." Sure, the visitations I was having were cosmic and outrageous and completely out of the realm of ordinary reality, but I didn't think of them as indications of grace in my life.

Once back in Eugene the expected thing for me to do was to re-enroll again in school, but school was not my goal. I wanted to be loose and unattached and ready for anything. I started hanging out, following my impulses. I wanted to see what would happen if I did not try to steer the ship of my life, but jumped into the current and allowed it to take me.

Yeah, I know, that's vague, but there is something to it. I had spent the last few years in a goal-oriented mode, a big percentage of my time focused on piano and music. I had a certain level of expertise I wanted to achieve, and I had achieved it. So that was done. Now I wanted something else, not so exact and definable as an ability to play an instrument, and I did not know how to go about getting it other than by following my impulses.

And another way to describe it is that something had grabbed my attention away from music, and I was taking a mini-break. I was still planning to put in time each day at the piano, but it was no longer an all-or-nothing obsession; it was a time for breathing out.

I'd known Marty and Douglas since my first summer in Eugene, when we were all just out of high school. They had also met each other that summer and fallen in love and had been together ever since, and now they were actually married.

They were living in a small house on the industrial side of Eugene, far away from the campus. The appeal of the property was that it had a large work shed where Douglas could do his pottery - he had a wheel - and the rent was much lower. It was good for him but not for her because they were so far away from the campus and from any kind of social life with their friends.

When Marty let me in she said, "Douglas will be out in his workshop for a while. Which is good, so we can catch up. Would you like some tea?"

"Sure," I said, "that sounds great."

I was also glad that Douglas would not be joining us for a while. I had a real connection with Marty and it was more superficial with Douglas. Talking with Douglas was predictable, hence, boring. Talking with Marty was not always pleasant, but it was always interesting, and sometimes emotionally challenging to me.

"Okay," she said, after we had our tea cups and were settled in the living room on a sofa, "Tell me all about why you came back. That was such a cool letter you wrote, and I want to hear more about it."

"Ah, okay, I can't remember what I wrote you in the letter, but..."

"I have it right here!" She reached over and picked up a book off the floor and showed me my letter, which she was using as a bookmark. "I have read it, I don't know, probably half a dozen times. I love your letters so much. I think Douglas gets jealous."

"Well, I did make sure to address it to both of you."

Marty laughed, "But he is not a reader. And he doesn't really get you, not the way I get you. You do know that, right?"

She stared at me, and I nodded my head. This was one of those challenging emotional times. She and I had made a real heart connection a few summers before, but in the present moment I was at a loss for what to say or do. I liked Marty, a lot, but she was married, and I didn't know what to do with the emotions she was stirring up.

"Okay, so, I had these experiences - the ones I wrote about in that letter - and I decided that before I do anything I need to figure them out."

"Before you do anything? But you came out here, isn't that doing something?"

"Yeah, it is, but I mean, before I decide to start a career or go back to music school again, or decide to go to school to study something else."

"So why did you think you couldn't do that back in D.C.?"

"Yeah, that was something I considered. Mainly because it's a big east coast city where people are either working or on drugs. And it's where I grew up and I know a lot of people there and my parents are there. Kinda hard to make a new start is what I'm saying."

She shrugged her shoulders and smiled. "Yeah, okay, I get that. Okay, so now that you're here, what are you going to do?"

"I don't know, that's what I will be finding out. That is the question. And for some reason I had the idea to start in Oregon. Probably because I really have had some amazing times out here."

"Sorry for changing the subject but I have to ask. Did you keep in touch with Alan?"

"Yes, I did see Alan. Not a lot, but, he is a good example of people I used to be close with who have gotten ... strange, or maybe they've just changed, and they are supposed to change, and that's the way it is, no one stays the same. Alan now lives out in the country a few hours from D.C. He lives with a woman, his girl friend, who I didn't really get to know. I think they were having a fight or something when I was visiting. I don't know what he does all day, other than he makes pipes, and shoots a bow and arrow. For some reason he's really gotten into shooting a bow and arrow."

Marty stared at me open-mouthed. "Are you joking?"

"No, I'm not. I know it's strange but I'm telling you he is into shooting a bow and arrow, like at a target, one of those big round targets."

She had a very disturbed expression on her face. "Wow, that doesn't sound at all like the Alan I knew."

"No, it doesn't. We had such great times living together at 518 (the address of a house we had rented together), and now I don't know what has happened to him. It's like D.C. or the big city or maybe it's the vibe on the east coast has put a spell on him. You get into strange things just to keep from going crazy. And then there is probably my closest friend back in D.C., Demetrius, who has taken too much LSD, and he has become a very strange guy who only wants to get stoned or drop acid."

I took a sip of tea, and Marty waited. "And I have another friend who only wants to talk about food. I mean seriously, he has become the manager of a health food store and so he works around food all day and when he gets home all he wants to do is plan and cook and eat a big healthy meal. And another friend who is now only into working at a tobacco shop. Selling pipes and cigars has become his passion. Weird!"

"Okay, so, you don't want to spend your life planning dinner, and you don't want to spend your life taking drugs, or shooting a bow and arrow, or selling tobacco, so what do you want to do?"

"I don't know but I've been reading some books."

"Oh good, tell me about the books you've been reading."

"Okay, well, one is by Fritz Perls, *Gestalt Therapy Verbatim*."

She reached over and took it off the book shelf. "Here it is! One of my favorites. Let's talk about it, whadja like about it?"

I was happy to see that she also had been reading that book. "Hmm... okay, well, he is able to uncover stuff in people that they didn't know was in there. And he does it in the moment, you know? Like, it takes place *now*, whatever it is that's fucked up in us, is in us right in this moment, now. And he does it through dreams, which is a way to look into what is going on beneath the surface. The idea that each item in the dream comes from the dreamer. Each person you meet in the dream is your creation, which of course is so obvious but still I had not thought about that until I started reading this book."

"Okay, so in the case of your dreams which you've been having, what does that mean?"

I was momentarily confused. "But wait," I said, "I don't see those as dreams."

And as soon as I said it I realized that it didn't matter. I could still explore the viewpoint of Gestalt Therapy which was that each aspect of the vision - or dream - came from inside of me.

I opened my mouth to continue, but Douglas had entered the house and had yelled out a greeting to me. Our conversation was interrupted. Douglas explained he had forgotten he had a meeting that night and that he could not stay for dinner. What meeting? It was only men, the group of men he met with, and they talked about men stuff. I was very curious about this, but he had to get cleaned up and leave, so we agreed to get together another time so I could hear more about it.

After he left I asked Marty, "So how is it with you and Douglas, being married?"

She answered in a surprised tone, "Well, ever since we met practically we have been living together, so in that sense absolutely nothing is different."

"Well, in that case why did you get married?"

She seemed surprised by my question. "But it's what we had always planned to do," she said, as if that was actually a valid reason. "And anyway, I want to get back to what we were talking about."

"Okay, then, I think what we were talking about was that in a dream each detail of the dream is seen as part of one's psyche. So, I had not considered my ... visions or whatever you call them, in that category."

"So, in what category do you place them?"

"I don't like the word vision either. It's not the right word to use because a vision implies something seen, and this was a full-body experience. I felt this thing touching me, I heard sounds, in fact, well, I did *see* things, like colors and lights, it involved all the senses."

"So would you say it was a spirit that visited you?"

"Yeah, that is, for sure, one way to describe it. I don't like that word either because something touched me, I mean physically I felt something touching me. So, how can a spirit also be physical? Anyway, I don't know how else to describe it. So, let's just say that a spirit visited me."

"So, this thing, this spirit did not have a physical body, or did you see its form or shape?"

"No, I didn't. I felt it, but I did not see it. When I closed my eyes I saw some outrageous colors and ..."

"Were your eyes open at any time during this experience?"

I hesitated. "I'm not sure, but I think they were at least some of the time. Well I know that at first my eyes were open because I was looking around the room and trying to figure out what had changed."

"So, something was in the room with you, but you could not see it?"

"Yes, something was in the room with me. That's what I definitely felt more than anything, was a presence of something in the room."

"And how about when it ended, was it similar to the feeling of waking up?"

"Yes, it was like I woke up."

"Well then, there you have it," Marty said, "I think you should look at it as a dream. An unusual dream, for sure, but still let's look at it as a dream from the point of view that every detail of what happened was actually a part of you."

I nodded my head, agreeing, but also wondering how exactly to do that.

She added, "My view is that everything in the world is really just an extension of me and how I view the world, so I don't think it matters one way or the other whether or not you call it a dream, or a vision, or a visitation, or a spirit, or all in your mind. It's now a part of your reality, and it's what you have to contend with."

I thought about this. I'd had this same discussion with a friend when I was seventeen, that the whole world doesn't exist outside of our own perception of it.

I said, "Look, I know what you mean, and it's all just words that we're using to describe something indescribable, but the way I see it is that there must be something greater than me because I don't have any memory of creating the world."

She peered at me. "Which leads us to the g word. Specifically, the g-o-d word."

I laughed. "Yep, we have arrived at the g-o-d word. Which I don't want to use, I don't want to actually say that word out loud."

Her eyes widened and she practically shouted, "But you do want to admit to something greater than you!"

I realized the idiocy of my position.

She then said abruptly, "Hey, let's smoke a joint. One of Douglas's students pays him in marijuana and it's really good."

She got up and came back with a baggie and some papers. "I've actually learned how to roll joints. You know I never used to get stoned with you guys when you'd smoke, but lately, I don't know, for some reason, I have been really enjoying it."

"That's because you have nothing else to do stuck over here on this weird side of town. I never knew about this part of Eugene."

"Very funny. And you are probably right. But I kinda like it. We did the unexpected, a thing I had not thought of doing before."

While she rolled a joint, I pondered whether or not to smoke with her. I had not told her I would not. It seemed like every friend I had in Eugene was into smoking and I had refused the offer a number of times since arriving. This time I was feeling like maybe I should relax my strict stance. So, I did.

As we smoked, Marty said, "This is the kind of conversation that is perfect for marijuana. So, let's forget about the g word for now and let's think about the uh… things in the dream. So, the first thing you felt was …" And she looked at me to fill in the blank.

"I was paralyzed with fear."

"Okay, so, that's good, a part of you IS paralyzed, is scared shitless. Unable to act, unable to do anything because it is afraid. How does that sound?"

"How does that sound? That sounds terrible! Not good. I don't like how that sounds."

"Yeah, I know that, but I mean do you think there's any truth to that?"

I took another hit and inhaled deeply. I knew for sure there was truth to that, and I had the thought that even with a supposed close friend like Marty, I was hiding something.

I said, "Yeah, I mean, for sure, there is a part of me that is … afraid."

In fact, I was starting to feel a familiar feeling of paranoia which can accompany a marijuana high, which was highly appropriate given what we were talking about.

She said, "Look, John, you obviously are a sensitive person. When you were living at 518 do you remember that time some people were over visiting, and there was a woman interested in you. She really came on strong. I mean she really dug you and she was aggressive. Do you remember that?"

"Uh, yeah, sure, of course I do." I was nervous about where this was going. I could feel my self wanting to sink into a hole and disappear.

"Okay, so from your … I don't know, lack of response to her, I would say that you acted like a scared rabbit."

Ouch, that hurt. And it hurt even more because it was true. I tried to come up with a response while she laughed. I couldn't.

"Can I ask you something?" Marty asked.

She went on since I did not have it together to formulate a verbal response, "Okay, well, I'll take that as a yes. My question to you is, why didn't you have any girl friends in those years we lived together at 518?"

I was not expecting that question. This was getting very confronting. I tried to think about how to answer that.

She went on, "I'm asking because that to me is an example of a part of you that is unable to act, paralyzed with fear. You know what I mean?"

I nodded my head. Yep, I thought, that's exactly right.

"John? Are you okay? You're not talking anymore."

Yes, because the marijuana was definitely making me paranoid. I sat up straighter and forced myself to say something, "I know, I'm uh… I don't know. I'm trying to think about your questions and what you are saying." My voice was sounding very far away and very weak. She went on.

"It's okay. We don't have to talk about this, ya know? But what about what I said about an example of a part of you that is paralyzed with fear? And in fact, speaking of Gestalt therapy, it's happening right now, isn't it?" She giggled.

I nodded my head, it sure was!

"I mean, Gestalt therapy looks at the moment and what happens in a moment to an individual's psyche. And right now, you look like you are … well, a scared rabbit. You know?"

Fortunately she said this in a very nice, sweet way. She was certainly having fun and enjoying herself.

She said, "This is soooo interesting. John? Please say something."

I stood up trying to break the spell I seemed to be under. "Yes, yes, I have not smoked in a while so ... maybe that's part of what's happening."

"Okay, so let's go on with your spirit visit. So, this thing comes into your room, you get paralyzed with fear, and then what?"

I forced myself to start talking. "Okay so, it's really like two feelings at once. I feel a presence in the room and I'm terrified, and the other feeling is an extremely pleasant feeling. There were these beautiful sounds, like footsteps shuffling on marble floors, and then as soon as I started to relax into that, a nice breeze starts blowing, my windows were open, and then the wind gets stronger and then it starts to massage the back of my head and my neck and shoulders, and it's a very nice feeling."

"Right!" She said excitedly, "And that is also you. You are that thing which is able to create beautiful sounds and feelings. You have that in you."

I tried to grok that. And I could not grok it. I said, "I don't really know how to think about that. Like, what does that mean?"

Marty looked surprised. "Are you serious?" Then she started to giggle.

I was feeling annoyed that she was so sure of herself, "So, I have a part of me that is beautiful sounds. Is that what you are saying? I don't know how to relate to that."

"Aren't you the one who's been learning piano so you can write music?"

I was stunned. "Oh. Duh! Yeah. Wow, that's weird I had not thought about that."

"Really? Well, you are the one who was hearing those beautiful sounds of feet shuffling on a marble floor, and voices echoing, you described it beautifully in your letter. That's what I immediately thought of, you as the composer, hearing beautiful music in your vision. Which sounds to me like a really cool sound."

I was shocked that this had not occurred to me; now it seemed so obvious.

Marty suddenly said, "Wow, you know, I cannot wait until I can get my license to practice therapy."

"You'll be good at it, you are already good at it. This has been pretty cool."

"I know. So, let's go on, that is, if you want to continue?"

"Sure, sure." My wave of paranoia had passed. "So, what happened after that was the wind turning into massage, some *thing* massaging me, but it also feels supernatural as if it is increasing the amount of presence in each moment. Because of course a breeze does not turn into a wind and then turn into a hand on the back of my neck. So, I was feeling overcome by a loving presence, and I was not able to calm down enough to enjoy it."

Marty grinned. "That seems too obvious. You are probably a great lover, you know, good with your hands?"

I had not response to that but felt I should say something, "I just wish I could enjoy the experiences, they certainly sound great as I describe them, ya know?"

"You know what? You need to meet my new friend, David. David Eisner. I met him in one of my psych classes. He's debating whether to become a priest or a rabbi. He's a cool guy."

"A priest or a rabbi? Why become either?"

"Go and ask him! I'm sure he'd love to tell you all about it, and I think you two would have a lot to talk about."

The evening ended shortly after that. I took the slip of paper with David's address on it and told her I would look him up.

Chapter 3

I needed to figure out where to live, and nothing I was checking into appealed to me. I wanted to keep my expenses low, and I also wanted some privacy and that combination was not easy to come by. 518 was too crowded and an old friend of mine, Charles, also needed to move out; so we decided to find a place together.

Charles had gone to college without a clue why he was going, other than to avoid going to Viet Nam, and had discovered photography, which became his passion and *almost* his entire life. He did little hanging out because he devoted so much of his time to photography.

On mornings when something particularly exciting was happening, he would be working in the dark room or he would have a class with his favorite professor, he would give a shout of unbridled joy when getting out of bed. I was happy for him, and in looking around at the number of people I knew, he might have been the only one who had such a clear-cut goal for his life that he was so happy about.

Charles was firmly in the camp of my friends who thought I was crazy and wasting my time. He had little curiosity about my search, and it was probably a mistake for me to move in with him. I did it for convenience. We found an apartment to live in which was spacious and gave me privacy since Charles was rarely there.

One morning I found in one of my pockets David's address, and I decided to take Marty's advice and visit him. He was a short guy with dark hair and twinkling eyes, and an overly-friendly attitude which eventually wore on me. When he heard Marty had sent me over to meet him, he welcomed me in. His living space was sparse, typical of the times, no furniture, some cushions on the floor, lots of books, records.

As we drank some tea, I started telling him about the experiences I'd had. His eyes got very wide and he said, "Your experiences sound so similar to what is described in a book I have been reading about Hasidic mystics. Before you leave I can loan you a copy. I have a bunch of copies cause I'm gonna use it in the class I am teaching on Martin Buber."

"Who is Martin Buber?"

He said, "You don't know who Martin Buber is?" He made an exaggerated show of shock. "Just kidding. Hardly anyone knows who Martin Buber is, but that's a good reason for you to come to the class I will be teaching. Then you can find out who he is."

I said, "You don't understand, I'm not enrolled as a student."

"I don't see that that matters. You don't have to be a student to attend classes."

"Oh, right," I nodded realizing that I had not considered that option. So, his invitation struck me as a real gift, and also the kind of thing I had been hoping to find.

He said, "We got off the subject. Your experiences sound so much like those of the Hasidim. Maybe you were one in a past life."

I shrugged my shoulders, "I don't know anything about them. David, Marty says you want to become a priest. Is that really true?"

"Yes, it is. I am considering it. The only problem is, I'm Jewish, so I think I should probably become a rabbi instead. It would be lot easier."

"But why? Not why would it be easier, but why do you want to become either one?"

David shrugged his shoulders and said, "Because I am drawn to that kind of life and because I feel it calling, it's called a calling when one knows one is supposed to go in a certain direction. It's something which is only obvious to you if you are the one feeling it."

He stopped talking, and I had no response to that. I was thinking my journey out to Eugene could be seen as a calling.

He went on. "I think a priest or a rabbi has the opportunity to do a lot of good in the world and be an inspiration to people, and people need that, they need inspiration."

"But if that's what you want to do - inspire people - can't you do it some other way than by joining an organized religion?"

"Yes, of course, and that's a question I have been wrestling with or maybe trying not to wrestle with it. I have not decided anything yet because I have not done anything yet. I realize there are other ways. But think of how huge the Catholic church is and how it is organized to help people all over the world. It does a lot of really important good works in places that have a real need."

I was inwardly shocked to hear someone say such a thing. In my view the Catholic church did equally as much wrong as it did right.

I said, "Oh, okay, so, you want to help people in practical ways ... that's different than inspiring people."

He nodded his head. "Right. Ideally I can do both."

"Okay, well, so what's the deal with priest vs. rabbi? Doesn't saying that mean you don't really believe in either one?"

"Huh? No, not at all, it means I believe in both! I like aspects of both. I think both have excellent qualities. You can disagree, but the fact is I do believe in both, I believe both paths are, quote unquote, true. Actually, I don't believe in truth with a capitol T, and I certainly do not believe it is confined to one path. Have you ever considered that maybe each religion is, or was at one time, a true path?"

I vaguely nodded my head, "Yeah, but what does that actually mean?"

David said, "Okay, good question. Now, let me ask you something, what did Jesus teach?"

I thought for a moment, surprised to be asked this question. "Well, I should be able to answer that. Let's see now. He taught to love your neighbor as yourself. He said if your enemy strikes you, then turn the other cheek. And, let's see, oh, that the kingdom of heaven is within. How's that?"

David was smiling, "Yes, excellent, those are things that Jesus taught. Okay, so then what does Judaism teach?"

I said, "Now that's a good question. I have no idea, you tell me. I had so many Jewish friends growing up. I went to a high school which was more than half Jewish, and I never knew what they believed in, other than their traditions. Light these candles to remember the night that we got out of captivity. Okay, that's great, but what does that mean you believe? I mean believe in, now?"

David smiled at me, "You know, you should become a priest."

"Hey, buddy, I take that as an insult." And then I laughed, trying to ease the impact my words might have. I felt a little embarrassed being so disdainful about something he was obviously seriously considering.

"Wait a minute though," I said, "I know what a priest believes in, but I don't really know what rabbis believe in other than their traditions. Catholics believe in Jesus, that he was the be all and end all, and Jews don't believe that about Jesus or anyone else right? I mean for them the Messiah never came, so are Jews actually looking for the Messiah to come again?"

He shrugged his shoulders. "Yeah, you know John, you're getting hung up on details. Forget about the details. I'm talking about something else. There's an essence to every religion. I could just as easily consider becoming a Buddhist monk or a Hindu holy man. I'm picking priest and rabbi because they are both common here in America which is where I live. There is a commonality to all the great religions and that's what I'd be inspiring people to tune into, not the praying to Jesus and Mary and all the saints and all that, or to the lighting of the candles and going to the temple as if by doing that you've accomplished what you are supposed to be doing as a Jew. Capiche?"

I was getting it, but I felt like he had never addressed my basic question, which I didn't need answered anyway, so I was gonna drop it.

But he went on, "Think of this, the first commandment that God gave to Moses was I am the Lord thy God, and you shall have no other gods before me. Think John, how you could inspire people if you could get people to understand that."

This statement really floored me. I responded, excitedly, "Well, I'd first have to be someone who understands that. And I don't think I do, I mean, what does that mean, anyway? Don't worship false idols? Our entire culture is based on the worship of false idols. So, looks to me like nobody is obeying the very first commandment."

He laughed. "Exactly! Okay, so what don't you understand about it? It means God is everything, John. It's a fact. If one focuses on the things of this world, one will be in a state of suffering. Only by focusing on God can one transcend suffering. And who really can focus on God all the time? I mean, who tries to?"

"Wait a minute, wait, wait." Now, I was getting more worked up. "That might very well be the case, I agree, but I want to know *how* that is done. How the hell do you focus on God all the time?"

"Aha, the million dollar question!"

"Well, how about giving me the million dollar answer then! You're the one saying you want to inspire people to do that! So, I'm asking you! How exactly do you go about focusing on God? I mean, is it doing the rosary all day long, praying twenty-fours a day or, I don't know, like, following a set of rules or guidelines? Or what?"

He smiled a beatific smile and shrugged his shoulders, which made me think he was basically bullshitting. He had no clue as to how one actually does it, he only knew that ,ideally, it should be done.

I suddenly remembered the book that had made such an impact on me, "Hey, have you read *Be Here Now*? It really says the same thing you're saying."

"*Be Here Now*? No, but I like the title. John, we have got to get together again, and soon. I have somewhere I have to go, but I have really enjoyed this."

"Okay, and next time I'll bring you *Be Here Now*."

"I'd love it, and I'll read you something, too. I'm serious about coming to my class, it just meets one day a week, and after this conversation, I know you will love it. Thursdays at 9 in the morning, okay? And let me get that book I want you to read."

The book he loaned me, *The Legend of the Baal Shem,* did have an effect on me; it placed my experiences into a framework I had not considered before. When I was a child my father had read out loud to me a book titled, *A Catholic Book of Saints.* Each chapter was about a different saint, and each saint had done something miraculous. The stories fascinated me, and naturally I believed they were true, since I was so young, and it was my father reading them to me and he said they were true, and in a child's eyes the father speaks the truth.

And also from a child's eyes, what is not possible? Obviously since there is a creation there must be a creator, and why shouldn't the creator bend the rules now and then and allow for certain people to perform miracles?

I'd heard that the Jewish tradition does not believe in saints, but this book describes the Hasidic mystics as having supernatural powers just like Catholic saints. The Baal Shem was a master living in Poland during the 18th century, and even though he was Jewish, the stories were not really about the Jewish faith. They were these far out stories of the Baal Shem knowing, for instance, who someone had been in a past life, and what they had done, and what they needed to do in this life. Very similar to the kind of thing Ram Dass's guru would know about someone.

When I say the book placed my experiences in a different context, I don't mean I now thought of myself as a saint, and I did not think of harnessing this power to perform good works, or bad works either. However, I did put two and two together and realize the saints must have been *experiencing* something.

Yet, I still had no interest in pursuing religion. The first fourteen years of my life had given me all the religion I'd wanted for this lifetime. And the stories in *Be Here Now* about Richard Alpert meeting his guru and getting a new Indian name were interesting to me, but still, I had to believe it shouldn't be that complicated and difficult. Laziness? Maybe, but still I had no desire to go to India and find a guru.

I was hitchhiking in Eugene, and a couple picked me up. They told me they could take me where I wanted to go, but first they needed to mail a package. It wouldn't take long. I said, sure. They got into talking about how to address the package because it was going to India and they were unclear about something in the address. I asked who they were mailing a package to in India. And they said with wide eyes and big grins, our guru.

I sat up straighter in the back seat of their car. "Really? Like, the guru in that book *Be Here Now*?"

They nodded their heads and smiled dreamy smiles. "Wow, what a far out book. Did you see him when he was here? Oh my god, he is so tuned in. Timothy Leary talked about turning on and tuning in, but Ram Dass did it, the only way you can do it, by going beyond ego, and without drugs. We were right up front. The vibration was so high."

"Is that your guru too? The one he meets in the book?"

"No, no, our guru is ___ "

I could not understand the Indian name they said. Then she added, "There is an old adage in India, when the devotee is ready the guru appears."

They were giggling like children as they finally decided how to write the address on the package and then they hurried into the post office and came out a few minutes later still giggling. Something about how they were acting turned me off, but I was not sure if I wasn't just jealous. I had no desire to mail packages to a guru in India, but I wouldn't mind feeling how they appeared to be feeling.

Not everyone I knew was debating whether to become a priest or rabbi, or was involved with a guru from India. One of my close friends in town was Bo Willy, who now lived at 518, the house near campus that I had lived in a few years back. He was sharing it with two other guys who also were in their last year before graduating.

Bo Willy was a fast-talking, cynical, Woody Allen-esque intellectual who loved to spar verbally with everyone about anything and everything. Being around Bo meant taking part in intellectual discussions on wide-ranging subjects: who is the best quarterback in the NFL, is Hesse more relevant today than Dostoevsky, who should win the academy award for best actor, who is the greatest blues singer, is Eric Clapton's talent trivial or significant, what's the best way to cook a burger. The more obscure the subject, the more passionate Bo became.

His parents had been sending him to a psychiatrist for years so he had a set-in-stone understanding of what his problem was. He actually considered himself an expert on what was going on inside himself even though he was an obviously tortured human being who was not comfortable in his own skin.

After trying to explain to him what I was doing, he got impatient.

"Cut to the chase, Kreilkamp, I know you have these wild dreams but what are you really looking for? I mean in the *real* world?"

"Ah, well, you could say I'm looking for a way to control my mind."

"Control your mind? What a fucking bullshit phrase, you're already able to control your mind. You can get up in the morning, feed yourself, make halfway intelligent comments. You wouldn't be able to have this conversation if you weren't able to, as you put it, control your mind."

"Oh come on, Bo, those things are not proof I can control my mind, those are automatic functions we do because we were taught to do them."

"Huh? Maybe we should argue that one, but anyway, okay, give me an example of how you don't have control of your mind."

"That's simple, when I'm tired, I lie down to sleep and I can't turn off the voices in my head. I can't just fall asleep even though I'm tired."

"No, no, no, you have it all wrong. You're just out of balance between your mind and body. It's a *physio*logical condition, not *psycho*logical. You have too much excess energy, that's all. Do what I do, go to the doctor and he'll give you something for that. In fact, I can give you some different things to try that I'm using."

"Bo, you're fucking taking pills because you can't sleep at night, but you won't admit that you can't control your mind?"

"Hold on, you mean to tell me, you're doing all of this spiritual soul searching just so you can get a good night's sleep?"

"Uhh… well, maybe! But no, not exactly, that's just an example, sort of like an immediate benefit I am hoping for."

"Well, then goddamit, tell me the real reason you're searching."

"Okay, another reason is, …" I was scrambling in my head for a reason. "I want to learn to meditate."

"Oh, please, god no! Meditate? You want to become one of those self-absorbed naval gazers? What good are people doing when they meditate anyway? It's the ultimate act of selfishness. You may as well be dead! You're adding nothing of value to the world. Sitting by yourself in the dark, what's that all about anyway?"

And so the conversations would go. Bo admitted though in more vulnerable moments that nothing terrified him more than trying to meditate, that is, sitting with his eyes closed, wide awake, with nothing to distract him from what his mind was thinking. And perhaps that's why he occupied himself with so many of the obscure details in the world.

He was a good friend though and turned me onto some interesting things, and he also taught me something about living the way you want to live. He was doing that. He was seriously going for whatever it was that was available. I especially admired how he shared freely his most intimate secrets. I was not able to be so free and easy with letting people know my emotional states.

Bo was not endowed with classic movie star looks. He was unusual looking, perhaps how an overweight Woody Allen might look, and women were not flocking to him, he had to really work for whatever attention he might persuade to come his way. And his efforts did bear fruit; a few girls did come over to 518 to hang out.

I was not impressed with one major source of frustration to him, Marian. She struck me as very uptight, and never really said much that was interesting or revealing. Bo's interest in her was a mystery to me, and I spent some time around her and tried to grok what Bo saw in her. And when I told him I did not understand his obsession with her, he responded convincingly.

"She's not real talkative, but that's not a problem for me. I like to talk, and she listens and seems to enjoy listening to me talk, so I don't care about her not talking. She's nice looking, you have to admit that. So look, the thing is, she's attractive, but either she's playing hard to get or she's a lesbian, or she's not interested. Pretty much flat out rejection whenever I make the slightest move in that direction...But what about you? Why aren't you going after someone like her?"

"Uh," there was more to the answer than I wanted to get into with Bo, but I said, "I don't feel that attracted to her, it's like there is a circuit that's not flowing or something. She hardly ever says anything that I find interesting. I mean, I know she does say some things, but very little and never anything revealing in any way. You have to admit that. I think she's boring."

Bo nodded his head happily. "Again, I don't have a problem with that. Why should she reveal herself to anyone who happens along her path?"

This made me laugh and was a classic Bo Willy line. It makes no sense if you examined it, but it sounded profound. "Okay, well, so that means you think there is something in there. All I'm asking is how come there is no evidence?"

"Look, Kreilkamp, I just wanna get laid. I don't care if she's the next Einstein or a simpleton. She's pretty. I want to make love with her. Period. End of story. And, by the way, what I asked is not why aren't you going after *her* but why aren't you going after someone *like* her.*"*

This was one of those difficult questions for me at that time, and when I hesitated he went for the jugular, "There's two possibilities that I can see. Either you're chicken shit," he looked at me over his glasses, which were constantly slipping down his nose, to gauge my reaction. "Or maybe your search for the meaning of life means you aren't interested in girls any more?"

"Look Bo, I have not had such good luck with girls, really since high school. It's been one disaster after another."

"Hey, join the club! What do you think, everyone else has found their perfect match? Name one person who does have a good relationship? Take Alan Montaigne. Now there's a guy who has always had a girl friend. Girls like him. He's attractive, he's smart, and he's always involved with someone. And each relationship he is in is worse than the last one. But at least he keeps trying."

"Yeah, well, then let's just say I'm not actively pursuing girls because I would rather be doing something else with my time. I mean if a girl happens across my path, then fine, but I'm not making any extra effort."

Bo shook his head in disgust. "Lame!" he shouted. "You're chicken shit, that's what I call that."

I didn't argue with Bo, I knew he might be right, but I also knew it might be something else. This might be an obscure connection and I didn't try to explain this to Bo, but at one time I'd lived at 518 with five other guys, and maybe it was because we were all born under the sign of Aquarius, but we all got along really well and did some cool things together, one of which was reading the same books and talking about them together. One of the books we all read that summer was *Autobiography of a Yogi* and we talked about it quite a bit.

That book was a straightforward description about what being an enlightened yogi is all about. Yogananda, the author, spells out what happened to him, and how it happened to him, and what it means in a practical way to one's experience of life to become a realized soul and to have cosmic consciousness. It never occurred to me when reading his book that he was making any of it up.

He proclaims loud and clear that a great and glorious experience is possible. But it takes something special, a special effort for sure, but more than an effort - there has to be some luck involved, or to use a religious word, grace is needed. My gut instinct told me that if luck - or, grace - was going to make an impact in my life I had to put myself into position to receive it. And that meant I had to turn away from the things that I had been wanting and making efforts towards acquiring, like girls.

It was fall and my friends and I loved to play football. We got into the habit of going to a nearby playground and playing a semi-organized game, and we also often threw the football around in the street.

One afternoon Bo and I were out in the street throwing a football and a guy with short hair wearing a tie approached us. I figured anyone wearing a tie was selling something, and I prepared myself to ignore him and whatever it was he was selling. He handed Bo a piece of paper and then headed over to me. He did not look like a salesman, so I figured he must be a religious fanatic, but at that time the Jesus freaks in Eugene dressed in the style of the original disciples of Jesus, long hair and ragged clothes. This guy came right up to me and said with a big smile and very intensely, "There is a secret inside you and if you know this secret then you will find true happiness and when everyone finds it there will be peace in the world." And he handed me a piece of paper. On it was a photo of a teenage guru from India and some kind of lecture about it.

I didn't know how to respond to this, but I didn't have to respond as he was already gone up the street looking for someone else to give a flyer to.

Bo called me over, he wanted to talk about it. "I've heard about this guy, this teenage guru from India. He came through D.C. last year."

"Yeah, I remember reading something about that." I did not mention my meeting with Jane and her daughter.

"Are you gonna go see him?"

I laughed, "Are you kidding? No way."

"Why not? I would think this would be the kind of thing you'd be interested in."

I was taken aback. "Uh, no, not really, I mean, a teenage guru? That's a little too absurd, and anyway, I'm not looking for a *guru*. Are you gonna go?"

Bo laughed, "Credo quia absurdum. Hell no, I'm not the guy searching for the meaning of life, you are. I figured you would want to check something like this out."

Theoretically, it seemed like I would want to check out anything and everything. But I didn't even consider going. My plan of action was to do what I felt like doing. If I didn't feel like doing it, I wouldn't. I didn't feel like checking out a teenage guru because .... well, because I didn't feel like it. Since I didn't even consider it, I'd just be guessing if I tried to explain my lack of interest. Maybe it struck me as cheating or too much of a short cut, or maybe it was that I did not want to be someone who was so desperate that I would go to a chubby teenager who drove a Rolls Royce and liked to eat ice cream. I remembered reading that about him in *The Washington Post* when he came to D.C. The article was called "Cooking with fruits and nuts." I didn't have any interest in becoming one of those fruits and nuts described in the story.

Chapter 4

David's class met in a space which was more like a dormitory lounge than a classroom. We were a small group, less than ten students, and we sat around in comfortable chairs and sofas.

David began the class by saying, "Hello, welcome to my class on Martin Buber. I am not interested in being the kind of professor who lectures to you, the students, who then take notes. I realize that for certain subjects that is appropriate, but for this subject I believe that all of you have as much to teach me as I have to teach you. Sure, I do know some things and I am looking forward to sharing my knowledge and understanding with you, but I consider myself an explorer on the path of understanding the miracle of life, not as someone who knows the path inside and out. And on this path anyone and any situation can teach me something. I welcome all of you to walk along this path with me. We will read from an unusual writer and thinker, Martin Buber, who wrote in his book, *I and Thou,* that the real magic and mystery in life is between people, between you and me, I and thou. So, with that in mind, let's get started. Let's go around and introduce ourselves, and when you introduce yourself say your name and a little bit about yourself and talk a little bit about what drew you to taking this class."

We went around the room and introduced ourselves. The other students were students who were taking this class to fulfill a certain requirement for whatever major they were seeking. No one else struck me as someone sincerely interested in seeking truth; however, I was struck by what a serious looking woman named Linda said, that she was interested in waking up. I was familiar with that term from *In Search of the Miraculous,* and I figured she must have also read this book.

After the class ended, I caught up with her as she was leaving.

"Hey, when you introduced yourself you said you are interested in waking up. What do you mean by that?"

She said, "I need to get to another class, but you should come to meetings I go to. They are on Tuesday nights at 7 in the Student Union. One of the things we talk about is what it means to wake up." As she was walking away, she added, "It's open to anyone, you should come. I think you'd like it."

I wrote that down in my notebook: Tuesday nights SU at 7.

There was also a yoga class being offered at the SU which I had been intending to check out. Yoga, in those days of the early 70s, was a mysterious word to me. All I really knew about yoga was it was something you did with your body so you could eventually contort your limbs and bend over backwards and stick your head through your legs.

In Ouspensky's book his teacher, G, claimed to be teaching the Fourth Way and referred to yoga as one of the first three ways to truth. There was the way of the fakir, the monk, and the yogi; and he said that a serious seeker of truth should be familiar with these three ways. I had noticed a poster advertising an "Introduction to Yoga" class at the Student union and decided one thing I needed to do if I was seriously seeking truth was to check out yoga.

From Yogananda's book I surmised that since yogis have supernatural powers, then yogis developed their supernatural powers by doing yoga. But that book really didn't get into details on the kind of yoga that Yogananda did. It was called Kriya yoga but it was never explained and didn't sound to me like physical exercises. I also did not understand the connection between having a loose, limber body and higher consciousness, but I figured it had something to do with mind over body.

When I entered the room, incense and candles were burning. Indian print cloths were hanging on the walls and colorful mats and pillows had been laid out on the floor. Two guys dressed in loose white clothing were sitting in lotus position with their eyes closed. I sat down on the floor with several other people who looked like newcomers.

One of the guys in white started the class with a fairly formal lecture about yoga and about the benefits of doing yoga. At various times in his talk his partner would read an appropriate section of a manuscript, which sounded like a manual from India for doing yoga. For instance, the first guy said that after doing yoga for an hour and holding each position correctly a person would achieve a "still mind." Then his partner read a section from the book that described the attributes of a still mind. For instance, a yogi with a still mind can sit for hours, undisturbed by worldly thoughts and desires. As his talk went on and more and more outrageous descriptions of the yogi state were described, the question rose in my mind, was he describing his own personal experience or his goal?

We did learn a few positions that night. The cobra was one I especially liked and did it regularly for years afterwards, but it was an intro and to actually learn the yogi positions required signing up for a 10-week course, which cost money. I balked at the cost. I had not been impressed with the presentation enough to spend my hard-earned, rapidly decreasing money.

However, I was curious, and I asked one of the guys after the class, "Are you able to experience those states you were reading about?"

He looked at me and then looked away. "It's a personal experience that cannot be described, words can never describe it." Then he looked at me, "Why don't you sign up and find out for yourself?"

I said, "Well, I'm not asking you to describe the experience, I'm asking do you *have* those experiences you read about from that book?"

The other guy had overheard my question and said, "That's not a fair question. You can't approach yoga like it's gonna be a drug trip or something. It's a practice, a discipline, and only by doing the discipline can you learn about what it will do for you. Would you like to sign up?" He was into being strictly business.

I should have probably walked away at that point, but I could not resist, "I'm not saying anything about a drug experience. I mean the experience you read about, having a still mind, are you able to have that?"

Maybe they were in a bad mood because nobody had signed up for their ten-week series, but the tone of voice in his response was nasty.

"I don't know why you are worried about whether or not we are having a still mind. The question you should answer is, do you have a still mind? We're offering a class on yoga that will help you develop a still mind, do you want to take it or not?"

I laughed. "Maybe later," I said lamely.

I didn't like how they didn't answer my question and anyway, the cost was too much. I was on a strict budget because I had a certain amount of money which I figured would last me about six months and I wanted to avoid working for as long as possible. That's what I told myself as I walked home that night, but really the reason was that I was turned off by their attitude and responses. If I had been attracted to their presentation, then the money would not have been a problem for me.

The next Tuesday I went to the meeting that Linda had invited me to. When I walked into the room at the Student Union about a dozen people were sitting quietly. I looked around and saw Linda and our eyes met, and she greeted me by saying, very seriously, "Well, I'll be damned! You finally dragged your fucking lazy ass over here."

I was shocked. Not what I was expecting, and I could think of no response other than to laugh nervously. My mind started to spin - had I promised her I would come last week? Where did she get the idea I had a fucking lazy ass? I glanced around the room and a few people were looking at her and a few people were looking at me. I found a seat and sat down.

It did occur to me later though that there was something about her greeting which might have been a playful wink from the beyond. Whatever that primal force was that had sent a non-physical entity to scare the daylights out of me and get me to move out to Oregon, and then arranged for Marty to introduce me to David and get invited to his class and meet Linda, and then have Linda invite me to this meeting, was telling me in no uncertain terms that there was no time to waste, let's get going!

The chairs were not arranged in rows but seemed to be randomly placed facing mostly towards the center of the room. A woman with long dark hair stood to one side bouncing a tiny baby in her arms. One guy with an open friendly face smiled at me with twinkling eyes, but everyone else seemed to be ignoring each other. We sat in silence until a man in a short pony tail started the meeting. He introduced himself as Justin, and his voice was soft and unassuming, not the typical voice of authority. "Hello, my name is Justin, for any of you who have not been here before."

Usually if someone is in charge of a meeting they make their voice unnatural in some manner to establish themselves as "in charge, " either to the audience or maybe to convince themselves. He did not do that, and I found myself leaning forward to hear better.

He continued, "We have these meetings to talk about what is going on, what is happening in each moment that we are putting our attention on. We are aware of something in each moment, but what, what is it that we give our attention to?"

He stopped and looked around.

Someone said, "The hum of the building's heating system."

Someone else said, "Biddy's smile."

The woman holding the baby said, "Biddy's heavy!" She sat down.

"The voice in my head telling me not to say anything."

Justin's face held no expression as he heard the various responses. I wanted to put in my two cents, what I was focusing on, just to say something, but he went on. "Working on oneself involves working on what one is aware of, where one is putting one's attention."

He had said the magic phrase *working on oneself.* This meeting looked to me like what I was looking for. I was all ears now.

"Last week we talked about experimenting with seeing how long we can hold our attention on one part of our body. For instance, if you are walking, then being aware of your right food going down. Or if you are sitting, being aware of your feet on the floor, or your back on the chair." He looked around the room as if inviting responses, and a guy with light-colored hair spoke.

"Yeah, well, I had the intention in one of my classes of my hands, to keep them on the desk and to keep them still. I did okay until class started and the professor started talking, and then ... forget it!" He laughed. "I could not hold the awareness of my hands and also be aware of what the teacher was saying."

Someone else said that when doing the dishes they wanted to be aware of the water touching their hands and after the first minute totally forgot about the experiment, and didn't remember until an hour after finishing the dishes.

Justin said, "It's important to recognize how difficult it is to follow through on what looks like a simple intention regarding our awareness. What if while you were doing the dishes someone was there reminding you?"

Someone spoke up from the back; I couldn't see who it was. "Like that mynah bird in the book *The Island.* It kept saying, 'attention, attention, attention.'"

I had read the book he was referring to, and I connected the dots. Trying to be here now. Here was my chance to contribute.

I said, "So, is working on oneself all about being here now? I mean, is that all there is to it?"

Justin looked at me and said, "Well, it's a big part of it, it's part of the goal, for sure. The first step though is seeing what are we paying attention to. What's in the way of being here now. For instance, let me ask you, just now, what was the topic of discussion?"

"The topic of discussion?" I asked. "Well, it was about how to be here now. Someone said something about the bird in the book saying attention ..." my voice trailed off. A few people giggled.

The guy with blonde hair said, "I think we were talking about how to remember, like, if someone was there reminding us, would it be easier."

Justin said, "My question was, would it be any easier if someone was there reminding you?" He looked at someone in the back of the room, "Did your comment about the book have anything to do with answering my question?"

The guy said, "Ah, well ... I guess not."

"No? Okay, so, why did you say it then?"

I could feel the guy squirming even though I didn't have a clear view of him, or maybe I figured I would be squirming in his position. "Uh, good question. It reminded me of something, you know, what you said, reminded me of ... the bird giving reminders to people to remember to be present, to be here now."

"Yeah. Well, okay then, how practical do you think it would be to use parrots?"

The guy said, "Not very practical."

Justin said, "What could be used instead of parrots?" Then he added, "That question is to anyone."

"Whew." The guy in the back let out a sigh and there was general laughter.

Linda spoke up, "I've tried putting notes to myself in my books, so during class I can be reminded. They help, sometimes."

Someone else started talking, but Justin interrupted, "So, why do you say they help sometimes? Why not every time?"

All eyes on Linda. I felt like I could see her brain spinning behind her eyes. "Well, because sometimes ... I'm too involved in what I'm doing. I see the note reminding me and ... well, I feel guilty is what I feel, I think, ..."

"On a scale of one to ten, in that moment when you see the reminder and you ignore it, how important is it to be reminded of your intention?"

Linda said, "Well, it's a zero."

"And yet you are the one who wrote the note to yourself. So how important on a scale of one to ten is that reminder to the one who wrote it and put it in the book?"

"Well, that's easy, a ten."

"Exactly. To that part of yourself it's a ten, to the one that saw it, it's a zero."

He looked around the room. Then he looked directly at me and asked me, "So what do you make of that?"

I was surprised to be asked but also pleased to be included. "What do I make of it? Well, that we're divided, one part of us wants one thing, and another part of us doesn't want it."

Justin said, "Yes, that's true, but I'm asking you, what do you make of that, what do you think of that? That one part of us wants one thing and another part wants another."

I felt stupid, "Oh, what do I think of it?"

Someone giggled. I could feel the eyes in the room and now I could feel my brain spinning. I struggled to come up with something. "Okay, well, that means ... that, at least some of the time, we really can't help ourselves. If we write notes to ourselves, we'll ignore them, so it's almost pointless to do it."

Someone else said, "And that means ... we're fucked."

General laughter. I relaxed and laughed too.

Justin said, "Yes, it does mean we're fucked if we are on our own and have no one to help us. And that's a very important point to realize. Right now, in this room we would probably all agree, or most of us, that we're fucked to try this on our own. But once you leave this room, once you leave this meeting, other parts of ourselves will take over, and will know nothing about this realization you are having now."

The meeting went on. Justin certainly seemed to know what he was talking about, and I liked listening to him speak. The ideas he was putting forth resonated with ones I had read about and had interested me. I associated Justin with Gurdjieff, but Gurdjieff himself had been so mysterious. It was hard to describe exactly what Justin was teaching, all I knew was that I liked it, and I knew I would come back, that this was a group of people I wanted to get to know better. I started coming every Tuesday night and became a regular.

Bo was taking a *Film as Lit* class, and he urged me to come. I was a big film buff so the idea of seeing a good film for free appealed to me. They way it worked was that the class would watch a film together, and then at the next class the professor would lecture about it. Listening to Bo rave about the professor's lectures inspired me to start seeing the films and attending the classes. The lectures were even better than Bo's hype had prepared me for. The prof took the movie-going experience to an entirely new level.

One aspect of his approach was that no detail in a film should be viewed as simply incidental or insignificant. Every detail in a film, no matter how small, was a conscious choice of the director, who was considered the author of the film. The director uses all the details in a film to convey his or her message, and by paying attention to the details the message becomes clearer.

After his lecture a second showing of the film would be scheduled for those students who wanted to verify the points made in the lecture. I started also attending the second showing, and I joined the small group of serious movie-buff students who would go afterwards to a café to discuss the film further.

While I enjoyed most of the films in the series, one film, *Panther Panchali*, by the Indian director, Satyajit Ray, affected me in quite a different way than the others. The film took me into a state of feeling, I felt myself in the scenes, no longer watching it with my analytical mind, no longer evaluating it, and trying to follow the plot, and trying to understand the subtext. Or trying to find the clues as to the deeper meaning of the film. I knew I was watching a movie, I didn't get so far out that I didn't even know I was watching a film, but I was deeply immersed in a feeling. The images on the screen of the Indian family in the rural village produced an overpowering feeling of ... something very beautiful. Love? Sadness? Beauty? Really an indescribable feeling, but I was right there with the family in the village, stooping on the dirt ground and looking into the eyes of the old patriarch of the family.

My sense of time was altered, I had no idea how long the film went on. The auditorium in which this film was shown had wooden seats, which usually grew more and more uncomfortable as the film went on, but this time I had no awareness of my body in the seat. And when it ended and the lights came up in the auditorium, I found myself unable to move. I had a strange urge to laugh hysterically or roll on the floor and weep. I opted to close my eyes. When I did finally open my eyes and get out of my seat, all my friends had left.

I caught up with Bo at the cafe. He was there was two new friends from class, Travis and Anna. They were in high-speed conversation mode, interrupting each other, talking over each other, dissecting the film in their usual manner. I sat and tried to listen and follow their ideas but found the feeling state from the film was still with me. I could not get that mental part of myself engaged to take part in the conversation.

Bo was talking about the recurring train image in the film and that one possible meaning could be the advance of civilization into the remote Indian countryside. Although he seemed to believe what he was saying about this, I was unable to latch onto it as interesting. The train whistle in the film had affected me so deeply, it had been one of the many impressions from the film that worked on my inner emotional state, overpowering me with the feeling. I wondered, what was it about a train whistle that can produce a sound so sad, so plaintive, so beautiful?

I blurted out, "No, forget about the train, it was the sound of the train whistle, the sound!"

Bo looked at me with disgust, "Yeah, like I said, the train, which would include its whistle, which is obviously composed of a *sound*. Thanks Kreilkamp, for clarifying that a train whistle is actually a sound! What would we do without you! Like I said, the train, including its whistle, signaled the end of the village …"

I tried to explain, "No, you don't understand, I'm saying the meaning is the feeling, or I mean the feeling is the meaning, which comes from hearing …"

But Travis had already interrupted Bo with his idea of the meaning contained in the recurring train motif and Bo was talking over Travis. Anna was looking at me with a funny look in her eyes.

I took no offense at Bo's words. I was too happy because I had just fathomed the strange fact that the feeling from the film was not going away. I was being buried under a flood of sensations. Who cares about meaning, anyway? What meaning is there in anything that does not also produce a feeling? And what meaning can anything have in comparison with the feeling it produces? The intellectual process of sorting out motifs and themes and symbols and meaning struck me as folly and inherently meaning-less, unless there was also a feeling.

Although my mental faculties could not get engaged, a different part of me was fully present and right there and fully engaged in sitting around the table with Bo, Travis, and Anna. The *it* in me was *feeling* the conversation, sensing the existence of something indescribable and mysterious behind the words that were being said. Each person was a manifestation of an inner person that none of us could see. And that while this inner reality was hidden, clues were erupting from each person with each change of expression in their countenances and each gesture. And then it hit me!

I laughed and proclaimed loudly, "Life is a film!"

This momentarily halted the flow of words from Bo, but without missing a beat, he went on, but did manage to throw me a disgusted and annoyed look.

I continued to laugh inwardly at my new-found awareness. How strange that life is a film, and here we are, sitting around a table, talking about *another film,* and oblivious to the fact that we are each of us in our own film.

I knew there was no point in trying to explain this. For one thing it would have meant stopping the intense back and forth repartee going on between Bo and Travis about *Pather Panchali.*

I had the distinct thought, I am now for the first time actually watching my life as if it is a movie! Everything going on around me was loaded with significance in the same way each detail in a film is significant. The body postures, the gestures, the expressions, the words being used, the glances, and what was *not* being said. And interestingly enough, the *content* of the words struck me as the least significant.

A film. My life is a film. The scene is the coffee shop, the Odyssey. The actors are all of us. The director is ...? Who is the director?

It was impossible to fathom it. How could there be a director? There were a dozen conversations happening all around us at all the many tables in this coffee shop, and this was one coffee shop in this small town. Thousands of different films happening in this one little dot of a town. And what about the other 300 million people in America? And the several billion people around the planet? Billions of films?

How could there be a director? How could a director be involved in this film, in my life? And also be involved in Bo's film, and Anna's?

Bo, Travis, and Anna were so preoccupied with their conversation that they ignored me and I was able to enjoy my unfamiliar perspective. I forced myself to stop my internal bewilderment and focus on the conversation again. I was immediately brought right back into the awareness of "this is a film," and it's a very interesting one!

Bo talking so brilliantly about the camerawork, was like a giant peacock, strutting around showing off his feathers, wanting Anna to recognize and praise him.

Travis was not really listening to Bo, just as Bo was not really listening to Travis. Travis was poised waiting for Bo to take a breath so he could launch into his own brilliant observations. And Anna?

The competitive juices flowing between Travis and Bo were not flowing from Anna. Something else was emanating from her, another world-view, another perspective. She was not trying to win in this discussion the way Travis and Bo were.

The talking was so fierce between Bo and Travis that neither one of them asked my opinion, and I didn't have an opinion anyway to share, so I was free to sit there and watch and feel and try to process their emanations. It was like I had a different kind of x-ray vision. I was not looking through their physical bodies at their skeletons, but I could see through their psychological barriers to what was really motivating them. The bottom line was that Bo was really just trying to impress Anna, and Travis did not seem to have an interest in Anna, but he clearly wanted to compete with Bo. So whatever Bo was trying to do, Travis wanted to beat him at it. And I could tell Anna didn't want Bo in the physical way Bo wanted her, and she had no sexual interest in Travis either; she was like a mother hen wanting to keep both of her chicks happy.

Bo and Travis were making so much effort to present something, and yet that *something* was really a smoke screen, hiding something else. Just like we wear clothes to hide our bodies, we use words, gestures, and expressions to hide what we are actually thinking and feeling. And growing up, becoming an adult, is a process of learning how to beat around the bush and play the game, to be polite, clever, sincere, funny, anything to avoid revealing what is really going on inside.

While I was fascinated by the films and lectures, and usually enjoyed the post- film discussions, what was happening in that conversation blew my mind and excited me in a brand new way. When I was observing the behavior of Bo, Anna, and Travis, there was no feeling of superiority or for the matter, separateness. It was more a pleasurable experience of feeling one with all of them. I knew Bo was trying to impress the female, and I knew that normally I would have had the same desire to impress an attractive woman.

It so happened that in that moment I was not in that specific desire, but in other moments I had recognized being motivated by the desire to impress Anna. And I also had the part in me that was like Travis, wanting to outwit Bo, to intellectually keep up with him.

Chapter 5

At the next Tuesday night meeting, most of the same people that had been there the week before were in the room. A woman named Sandra read something she had written in her journal about an experiment she was doing, that if she passed a church she would go into it, at least for a few minutes.

Something about that struck me as really cool and also significant. I thought, what an amazing thing to do during one's day, to go into a church, for no reason.

Someone asked the obvious, "What do you do when you go into the church?"

"I go in and look around, sit down for a few minutes ..."

She left the sentence hanging there. Either Sandra was extremely nervous or she was naturally a vibrant human being, and I mean literally a vibrant human being. Her voice and even her face seemed to be slightly, very slightly vibrating, as if there was an underlying nervousness running through her.

She was continuing to talk and I was trying to follow; she said something like firing orders getting interrupted, and Justin said sternly, "Sandra, speak English."

She looked startled for a moment, then she collected herself using what looked like a force of will and said, "Oh, okay, yeah, I mean, I normally, you know ..." she was searching for the words.

"Okay, so, if I'm going to the store, I want to get to the store, stopping and going into a church along the way is not what that part of me wants to do. It wants to get to the store, it does not want to go into a church. And then, uh, ..."

Justin said, "Good, you said it in English, you don't need to go on."

Someone asked, "Did you pray?"

"No, no, just stop and go in. That's all."

"I don't get it, what's the point of that, I mean what does it have to do with anything?" asked a frowning woman who I had not seen the week before.

"Well, like I said, I was able to see that one part of me did not want to go into the church. It wanted to do what it wanted to do, which was get to the store and then get home."

The woman was clearly not happy at this answer, as her frown continued moving into different shapes on her face.

Sandra continued, "I was raised Jewish and I've hardly ever been into churches, and I mainly noticed all the art work, and the crucifixes, the candles. I wondered mostly about the crucifixes. Why is it so important for Christians to remember that Jesus had died on a crucifix?"

Of course I knew the answer - since I had been raised in a Christian religious family, and I spoke up, "Jesus dying on the cross opened up the doors of heaven so people can now go to heaven when they die."

This sounded so ridiculous coming out of my mouth, even though it was of course what I had been taught. I still felt a little bit foolish proclaiming such a thing.

Sandra laughed, "The doors of heaven? Wait a minute, you mean, there's actually doors to heaven?"

The friendly guy named Tuck said, "Yeah, they are right after you go up the 'stairway to heaven'."

People laughed, and I added, "You know, the pearly gates! Where St. Peter hangs out. You've heard about St. Peter, right?"

"St. Peter? Of course, but I mean, I've always assumed that no one actually believed that, you're saying that is the reason Jesus died? It sounds so ridiculous." She giggled.

A guy named Michael said, "That's also what I was taught. Jesus died so people can go to heaven after they die. Forget about the stairway or the gates or St. Peter, all that's a nice story or metaphor."

Linda interjected, "It has to do with sacrifice. God - the father - had to sacrifice his son - Jesus - so our sins could be forgiven."

I added, "And so the crucifix is the most powerful symbol in Christianity. It reminds Christians what Jesus did for them."

At this point Justin stood up and drew a cross on one of the blackboards in the room. We all looked at it and waited for him to say something about it. But he didn't say anything, he just sat down again after drawing it.

Then he spoke, in a quiet voice, so again I had to lean forward in my chair to make sure I didn't miss a word, "The symbol of the cross consists of a horizontal line and then a vertical line. Let's suppose the horizontal line represents ordinary life. What would you say ordinary life consists of, for us?"

I could feel my brain shifting gears. He was taking this into an entirely different direction than we had been going, which was trying to explain Christianity to Sandra.

Someone said, "Going to school to learn something so you can have a career and make money."

Justin told someone named Rob to write the suggestions on the right-hand side of the board.

Rob got up and dramatically drew a huge dollar sign, which got some laughs.

Tuck said, "Yep, that pretty much covers it!"

The woman with the small baby in her arms said, appropriately, "Raising children."

Rob wrote *kids*.

Someone else said, "Watching TV."

"Going to movies."

"Buying a house."

"Traveling."

After some more suggestions, which Rob wrote on the board, Justin said, "So, you could say the horizontal line represents the ordinary aims and dreams of most of our lives."

Frowning woman spoke up, "I don't think I have an ordinary life, and I don't think I have ordinary dreams."

Justin said quietly, "Okay. Listen first to the rest of what I will say and then let me know if you agree or not, okay?"

"Well, so far, I don't agree."

"Right! I got that. But wait till you hear the rest, okay?"

He went on. "Even if we want to become the greatest musician or the greatest lawyer or the greatest whatever, that dream is within the framework of life as we know it, say, in our American culture. We have famous musicians already, so someone wants to become another one. It's certainly nothing out of the ordinary, it's repeating something which someone else has done. We have plenty of famous and rich lawyers, so maybe you want to follow that same dream. All of that takes place on the horizontal line. And maybe one way to describe ordinary is to say that it has a repetitive nature to it. It is repeating what either you have done or what someone else has already done."

Justin stopped and looked around the room, as if inviting comments or questions.

Frowning woman said, "I just don't like the word ordinary. It's like you're putting down everything people are involved in, and I don't see why you have to put them down. People are doing some far out things. I don't care if it has been done before. Everything in the world has been done before. There is nothing new under the sun. Something can be special and incredible even if it's been done a million times before. I don't know why are you calling it ordinary."

Justin replied, "Okay, well, let me explain more about what I mean by ordinary. Ordinary in the sense of what that dream can deliver to you; or to put it this way, what you will become or how you will change once you achieve your dream. Which is, in my opinion, that you will not change at all. And I understand that is a radical claim. But that is what I am saying. Doing things on the ordinary plane will not change you. Nothing will change in you. You will not become anyone new, you will not change in any significant way whatsoever. You will still be the same fucked-up person or maybe un-fucked up person you were before. You might have a PhD or a Master's degree or a lot of money or a big house, but you, the inner you, will not have changed one iota. Our culture has produced so many extreme examples of people who achieve fame and then we find that their personal lives are hell, so we don't need to get into proving that.

"And here's another way to think of it: the horizontal line is all about circumstance, changes in the externals. The vertical line has *nothing at all* to do with external circumstances. And on the horizontal line you have your preferences, you like this, you don't like this, you pursue this, you run away from this. But those changes in the external circumstances do not mean that anything in you is changing. And what we are interested in here, or rather what I am interested in pursuing, is making a change inside that will then make the external circumstances meaningless."

Michael asked, "So, you are saying that the horizontal line is all about external circumstances, and that the vertical line has nothing to do with external circumstances. So, what does it have to do with?"

Frowning woman spoke up, "I so disagree with all this. I think that if I pursue what I am pursuing, which in my case is theatre, then I will change. I mean I already have changed, and of course I will continue to change. And it is inside that I am changing. Because I have a greater understanding of the subject I am studying and that by doing something and going after something I will become a different person than I was before I started."

Justin responded, "Okay, I know exactly what you mean. You will become a better actress, you will have a greater understanding of theater, and all that is needed to produce plays, etc. I understand that. In that area of your life you will change, but I maintain that it is circumstantial. Your understanding and knowledge of theater will be increased …"

She interrupted him, "And I - me - who I really am - will also change because of what I have gone through in becoming a better actress."

Justin said, "I think I need to define the vertical line and maybe then what I am saying will make sense to you. So, let's talk about the vertical line. If the horizontal line represents everything that's being done every day in our society or in our culture, then what does the vertical line represent?"

Silence. I was enjoying following his words and his reasoning but was having a hard time thinking of an example.

Rob said, "What is possible?"

Justin responded, "You have to be more specific than that."

Linda said, "God consciousness."

Justin indicated for Rob to write that on the board.

Justin said, "It's important to be able to say at least in a general way, what it is you are shooting for."

He turned and looked directly at me, "Why did you come here tonight?"

I thought about it. "Because you are talking about something here that interests me."

I realized I needed to say more than that. "I think we are talking about how to wake up. Or to find out how to wake up. I am asleep, or it feels to me like I am asleep because so much goes on that I am not aware of. So I want to learn how to become more conscious, more aware in each moment. So maybe I came because I am hoping to learn how to be more aware."

I then decided to take a chance. I looked at frowning woman and said, "I am trying to become a musician, and I can tell you that no matter how good I get at playing the piano, me, I, the thing inside my head looking out my eyeballs, is not changing. I'm gaining a skill, but I am still the same person inside."

Frowning Woman shrugged her shoulders. "Nonsense! By learning to play an instrument, you will also change. Of course you will, you will become more disciplined, and more aware of the nuances that make up music, your ear will develop, I mean if you really pursue learning music how can you not change?"

I started to answer but Justin intervened, "Okay, okay, I want to talk about the vertical line now. Michael, how about you, why are you here tonight?"

"I want to find out what is real behind this illusion of our senses."

Justin nodded his head, "And you?" he asked a woman I had not heard speak before.

She said, "I think he said it for me." She pointed at me.

After hearing from a few more people, Justin said, "We know how to make a change on the horizontal line. Let's think about how to make a change on the vertical line. But how do we make a change on the vertical line?"

"LSD."

Justin wrote drugs on the board.

Someone said, "Meditate."

"Practice yoga."

"Pray."
"Fast."
"Read books."
"Search for truth."

Justin was writing these down on the board, and he turned and said, "How do you go about searching for truth?"

Everyone looked at Linda who had said it, and Justin said, "I'm asking all of you, not just Linda."

I said, "How about coming to meetings like this one."

Justin said, "What makes you think you will find truth here?"

"Well, because you are talking about stuff like horizontal and vertical lines and giving a different perspective than any I have heard anywhere else. It seems like it's headed somewhere different than anything else I've come across."

Justin then asked, "So, what is your responsibility in the search for truth?"

Then he added, somewhat repetitiously, "That's for anyone to answer."

Rob said, "To try to look beneath the surface." Then he added, "and to have my bullshit detector turned on."

People laughed.

Justin said, "Yeah, the bullshit detector is essential, that's for sure. What else? What else is your responsibility?"

"To question what you say, or what anyone else says. To not just accept everything that's said in here as the ultimate truth."

Justin nodded. "Very good, to question."

As the meeting continued, I could not tell what Justin knew or did not know, but after the meeting I felt very energized, and my bullshit detector had not gone off once. I knew I'd be back for more.

The next movie the class watched was *La Grande Illusion*, a French film about the idiocy of war.

I sat near Bo and noticed that he was taking copious notes during the screening. Afterwards at the Odyssey, while we waited for Anna to bring her pot of tea to the table, he half-sheepishly and with obvious pride pulled out his notebook and showed me all the pages he had scribbled on during the film.

"I got carried away with possible references to illusions, they are like everywhere in the film."

I asked, "What about what he said about watching the film the first time as a movie-goer?"

The prof had emphatically made the point that the auteur of the film created the film for someone to see, not for someone to study. So, he said, before you can study a film you must first see the film the way the director intended it to be seen, as a regular movie-goer, not as a student of film. In other words, don't take notes when you first watch the film.

"Oh hells bells, man, rules! Who needs 'em? I don't agree with that. I don't see why I can't appreciate the film while I am also analyzing it. That's how I do things, I analyze, that's how I appreciate things. Seems to me that the more attention I am paying to the film, the more I will appreciate it. I know he's like a god of film but that doesn't mean that everything he says is right."

Anna arrived and put down her tea pot. Bo subtly held up his pages of notes for her to notice.

Anna didn't say anything but she pulled out her notebook and showed the notes she had made, ruffling through a number of pages with writing on them.

"Wow," I said, "I think that's even more than you, Bo."

Bo said, "Wait, wait, that might look like more but you can't go by the number of pages. Look, you have hardly anything on each page. Let's go by lines."

Anna gave him an anguished look, "Robert, I am not counting the lines! I refuse to fall victim to your twelve-year-old competitive nature. Grow up!"

I laughed, and Bo laughed too. I was impressed that she was calling him by his real name. Maybe she really is interested in him. Bo had been talking about her in very hopeful terms lately.

He said, "Come on, don't take it personally, I do it with everyone. Just like I analyze, I also compete, it's who I am. It doesn't mean anything."

She said right back, "Well, have you ever considered maybe changing?" Wow, I thought, she's giving it to Bo the way someone should be giving it to Bo.

"And what do you mean, it doesn't mean anything? Of course it *means* something, it means you are trying to prove yourself as better than me - or whoever happens to be with you - because you are so insecure."

She stared at him. He looked uncomfortable and shifted in his seat. I had never seen Bo look so submissive. Maybe he'd found his true love, a mother figure.

She went on, "If you can win at this - have the most number of notes - then you will feel good about yourself."

He looked like he was trying hard not to say something. He kinda shook his head and shrugged his shoulders at the same time, indicating something ambivalent, finally muttering. "Of course that's true, I mean, I already knew that."

Anna said with a wicked smile, "I know you know that, but now you know that I know it. And I am not gonna put up with it." Then she said, very sweetly, "Would you like some of my tea, Robert?"

"Yes, thanks." He smiled at her, grateful she was moving on.

"Okay, okay, why don't you go first, what's the first thing you wrote down?"

I said, "But wait a minute, Anna, how can you take notes on a film you have never seen before? How can you watch if you're writing?"

"I have seen it before," Anna said. "Twice! So I figured it was okay."

Bo grinned, "I admit, I saw you taking notes and I figured I had to also take notes. Can't let you get ahead of me."

As soon as the words were out of his mouth he realized what he had just said. He shrugged his shoulders, "Sorry." Then his face flashed for a millisecond into a weird, wicked smile and then immediately settled back into a passive, meek expression towards Anna.

He thought of something, his face brightened, and he said, "Oh, Jackson said he would come for dinner next Tuesday night! And he's bringing his woman. Cassandra is her name by the way." He looked a bit proud that he knew the name of the glamorous woman who'd been seen at the films with the famous celebrity film professor, Jackson.

Bo asked Anna, "You are coming, right?"

Anna said, "Of course, I would not miss that. Who else is coming?" She looked at me.

Bo said, "Well, not Kreilkamp. I already talked about it with him. He's got something better going on. Travis, and Andy will be there. And maybe Charlotte, I will invite her the next time I see her. So that's seven of us, which I think is enough."

Anna turned to me and asked, "Why aren't you coming?"

I suddenly realized my decline of Bo's invite meant that I would have to explain to her my other interest. She knew I was not enrolled as a student, but she had no idea what I was doing.

I said, "I go to meetings at the Student Union on Tuesday nights."

She asked, "What meetings?"

I said, "They're led by a guy named Justin. He talks about a new way of looking at life, from the point of view of studying one's self. Paying attention to what one is doing, thinking, feeling at all times."

She said, "Is that sort of a psychology discussion group?"

I said, "No, not really, but, well, maybe. Sort of a lot of things, hard to describe. It's different each time I go, but mainly it's about how to know yourself, learning how to pay attention to what you are doing on another level. Like, say, you have your notes out, you are talking to me, are you aware that you are stirring your tea with your spoon?"

She looked down at her tea cup as if she'd had no idea she was stirring her tea.

"Well, sure, I knew, of course, on some level I knew. My hand knew because my hand was doing the stirring. But so what? It's so dull and uninteresting. Why would I want to put all my attention into stirring my tea? It's so much more interesting to be aware of you and Robert and what we are talking about. And then my tea can also get stirred."

She smiled, pleased with her answer, and went on. "We are functioning on so many levels all the time anyway. How can we be aware of it all? Our heartbeat, our pulse, our body temperature, the chairs we are sitting on, the temperature in the room, the sound of the rain outside. Even though, as you say, I am not aware of it all, on some level I am aware of it, that's why I'm able to say all the stuff that is happening, but I can't focus on each thing; otherwise, what kind of conversation would we have anyway?"

She paused. "Is there something wrong with that?"

Hmm... I was not sure anything was "wrong" with it, but I had to say something. "I know what you mean, but what about thinking of it this way. It's interesting being aware. I mean, awareness itself is interesting. And the more you can be aware of yourself, I mean aware of everything about yourself then the more interesting each moment is."

Her face went into an "aha" expression, and she stated definitively, "You're an existentialist. I didn't realize that about you."

Bo said, "I've told him that so many times!"

"You have? When?" I asked. I didn't remember Bo calling me an existentialist.

"Oh fuck'n A, man, come on! The other night with Andy, remember? Listening to Coltrane?"

Anna said quickly, "Robert, who cares if you had already told him that? Are you competing again?"

Bo rolled his eyes. "Okay, jeez, I'm sorry, I'm sorry. I wasn't really competing. I was making the point that I had already told him that."

"And you had to let us all know that you had thought of it already?"

Bo threw his hands up in disgust. "Okay, okay. It's in my blood, what can I say. Anyway, let's forget whether I already knew that, do you agree with it, Kreilkamp? Do you agree you're an existentialist?"

I shrugged my shoulders. I was feeling frustrated that what I was saying was coming out in such a way that Anna's only response to it was that I was an existentialist.

"God, I don't know, I guess it makes sense. I believe the most interesting thing is that I exist in this moment, right now. I've forgotten, is that what an existentialist believes?"

Bo was getting impatient and said in a whiney voice. "I want to talk about the movie."

"Wait," I said, "Anna, and you too Robert, why do you have to come up with a label for what I'm doing, or thinking, or believing? The important thing is what I am doing and thinking and believing, not the label you put on it."

Anna peered at me, "Why don't you want to be an existentialist? There's nothing wrong with being an existentialist." And then she stated with authority, "And anyway a label is not a limitation, it's a ... direction. I know what direction your thoughts go in, and that's useful for me to know in understanding you."

I had no idea how to answer that, and in the moment of silence, Bo interjected, "I am now picking up my notes, and I am looking at them, in full awareness. And I am thinking, Anna, what is the first note you wrote?"

Anna smiled, "Be patient, Robert. So, John, you would rather go to a meeting about ... that, whatever it is ... then come and have dinner with the guy who is an absolute genius when it comes to understanding film. That surprises me. I thought you loved film as much as we do."

I thought it was cool that she was recognizing the importance of my decision. It had surprised me too. When Bo had first told me about the dinner and had asked whether I wanted to come, I had said sure, but then he had said it was on a Tuesday night, and I was disappointed, but I also knew I did not want to miss Justin's meeting. Bo had pointed out that I could go any week to Justin's meetings, but this dinner was only gonna happen once. I still held firm. I had moved out to Oregon to find something more than a great discussion about film.

"I have a different priority. You guys are students, I'm not. I'm looking for something else, I'm not exactly sure how to describe it other than I want to unravel the mystery, the mystery of existence."

Anna looked at me thoughtfully.

Bo didn't. "Okay, okay, that's all something I have heard before, mumbo jumbo, the search for the holy grail. The thing is, what you are talking about, can also be done through something like studying film."

He added, nodding at Anna, "Or studying Russian. Or anything you do, depends on how you do it."

Bo could sound so wise, and how could I argue with that?

I responded, "I know what you mean, and you might be right, but I think it is different. I'm not saying I don't enjoy doing stuff like going to films and talking about them. I do enjoy it. It's just not …" I stopped, I was feeling frustrated trying to explain this.

Anna abruptly turned to Robert and said, "Okay, Robert, my first note?"

And they were off and running comparing their notes. I soon bid them good night and left them to their frantic, intellectual pursuits. I could not keep up with them, and I was happy to be left behind.

Chapter 6

One day we were throwing a football around in the street when an old T-bird stopped beside me and honked. I looked in and saw someone I had not seen in years, Lance Miller. He pulled over and parked and jumped out of the car and greeted me with a wicked grin.

Lance had been one of my first friends in Oregon. He'd lived on the floor above me in the first dorm I'd lived in, and he was a very different person from the other students I met that summer. For one thing, he was much older, and most of us were just out of high school. I never understood what he was doing there; he had no interest in school, never did any work, and from what he told me he was failing everything. He also took medication, which I gave no thought to and didn't connect the dots that the pills must have been for a psychological condition and not a physical one.

I had gone to visit him at his home a few years after that summer and had been shocked by what his life consisted of. He lived with his mother in a small house in a small town in Oregon. And when I arrived in the middle of the afternoon, he and his mother were watching TV together.

We then had gone to Portland together to visit some of his friends, and it had not gone well. Hitchhiking home with him, we had gotten a ride from someone who was carrying a bag of coins in the back seat. Lance had wanted me to steal either the entire bag or at least some of the coins. I refused to do that and after the driver had let us out, Lance was super pissed when he found out that I had not taken the coins.

He had no sense of gratitude to the driver for picking us up, and in that moment I figured I would never seek him out again.

I had told Charles about that visit after it had happened, and so now in the present time when Charles found out I had invited him over, he was stunned.

"John, are you crazy? You invited that psycho kleptomaniac over to our apartment? I'm holding you personally responsible for everything I have of value. If anything's missing, you will have to replace it, and I'm serious, man!"

I had really nothing of value in the apartment, but Charles had parents who fully supported his college career so he had lots of nice, valuable stuff, like a really great stereo, and a record collection, and big beautiful photography books.

I said, "Oh come on, Lance wouldn't steal from us, we're his old buddies."

Even as I said it I had my doubts. And it did give me pause and make me wonder why I had invited him over. Perhaps because I was in this mode of taking any opportunity to experience the new, unusual, and unexpected. The Fool mentality. If it would be good for me was irrelevant. My goal was to be open to anything. I figured I would certainly find out something interesting talking to Lance, an insight into a mind very different from my own.

And then again maybe it was the unrealistic dreamer in me. I held out hope he may have changed. Lance had been with me the first time I got off on acid, and because of that time we spent together I thought he had a deep side. I wondered about that though; maybe it was all in my imagination. I had experienced some profound insights and experiences with him, but what had he experienced?

For instance, that night on acid, we had stood in front of wall-length mirrors which were at the entrance to the dorm, and we stood there for quite a while. I have no idea how long, other than that a number of people came in or left while we were standing there. I had never stared at myself so long and so unabashedly and without judgment. I fell in love with myself and with Lance too.

Now, in thinking about it I realized I had no idea what Lance had experienced. My assumption that he was feeling the same things I was feeling was probably wrong.

He came over and we sat together in the living room, and it did not go well from the start. He seemed nervous about something, maybe the fact that our apartment looked nice - because of Charles' stuff - and maybe he was feeling intimidated by it. And then my heart sank when he pulled out a bottle of Scotch and said, like we were in an old west saloon, "How about getting us a couple of glasses?"

I got up and returned with one glass.

"What the fuck, man, one glass?"

"Yeah, I'm not really in the mood to drink."

"What are you talking about? You're not gonna drink?"

I said, "No, and I don't smoke either anymore, none of that stuff, clutters up my brain."

I could have kicked myself for adding that phrase, 'clutters up my brain,' because he took that personally as an insult.

"You think my brain gets cluttered from drinking? Just the opposite man. I feel alive when I drink. I can think very clearly. Yep."

I tried to change the subject and asked him, "You said you are passing through, so where were you coming from?"

"Aha, you're trying to change the subject. And the subject is …." and he held up, very dramatically, his bottle of whiskey.

He took a big swig and put the bottle down in front of me, indicating for me to take it. Then he added, "Las Vegas," as he leaned back in his chair.

"Really, Las Vegas? What were you doing there?"

"What was I doing there? Shit, man, I *live* in Las Vegas. Yeah, I live in fucking Las Vegas, that fucking no good town."

He pointed at the bottle. "Come on man, have a drink with your old buddy, Lance. Don't be an asshole about it."

I ignored him and said, "What do you do in Las Vegas?"

He scoffed. "What do I do there? Nothing. Fucking nothing. I don't do a fucking thing in Las Vegas. Other than drink and gamble, and lose a shit load of money. Have a drink, motherfucker."

At this point I realized I needed to get him out of the apartment at soon as possible. If we was now gonna call me motherfucker, nothing good could possibly come of this visit.

I got up. "Hey Lance, maybe you should go. I'm not into drinking, and you seem to really want someone to drink with you, and I'm not gonna do that."

He said, "Fuck man, I ain't leaving until we finish this bottle. Sit down and have a drink, man. Come on, remember, we're friends! Take a fucking drink."

He took another swig and again put the bottle down in front of me. "Drink!"

I did nothing.

He pulled out a knife and showed it to me. "Do you see this? This is a fucking knife, man, and it can do some bad shit to someone. I'm warning you now. Take a drink!"

I don't know what I was thinking because there really was no time to think. I instinctively refused though, and this time he stood up and leaned across the coffee table and held the knife at my stomach.

"Hey you, you don't want drink in your stomach, how bout ..." He paused dramatically. "Or this knife?"

He had a very evil grin on his face.

My worst fears had materialized. Lance *was* a psycho and he had a knife and he had it just a few inches from my stomach. I also knew though that I had no choice. I could not submit to this maniac.

I said with a pretty good show of nonchalance, almost like I was bored, "Lance, come on! Really, you should go."

Inside though I was bracing myself for his attack and wondering what the hell to do if he actually started to thrust the knife at me. I was as far from being a fighter as you would ever find.

Then something unexpected, and very welcomed by me, happened. Lance started to cry. He put the knife on the table and sat back down in his chair and started to bawl.

"I'm sorry man, I'm sorry. What the fuck am I doing? I'm gonna stab my old buddy, John? Why? I'm a fucking loser, man. I'm a fucking no good asshole. I should fucking kill myself, man."

Relief flooded me, and I said, "Hey, Lance, it's okay, I forgive you. It's okay, I really didn't think you were gonna do anything to me."

"I'm a fucking coward man, I'm a fucking no good chicken shit coward. You know what I do in Las Vegas, man? I rob women, old women. Yeah, I rob fucking old women, I take their purses, I hold up old women! I hide out in the shadows by the motels and when an old woman is walking alone at night, I'll hold her up. If there's two of them I don't have the guts! That's what I do man, I'm a fucking no good loser."

He was holding his head in his hands, his shoulders shaking.

"I'm gonna get the hell out of here man, you don't want a fucking no good loser like me here."

He stood up. He picked up his knife and put it in his pocket while he continued to berate himself, "Sorry man, for ruining your evening, I'm such a fucking coward, I'm such a fucking asshole."

I had no response. I wanted to offer him some comfort but I also did not want to extend the visit. And so I offered my hand to him and said, "Hey man, I hope things get better for you. I wish you the best."

He left, and I locked the door and sank to the floor. My heart was pounding. I heard his car drive away and decided to go for a walk around the neighborhood. I needed to clear my head of Lance Miller with his whiskey bottle and knife.

The night was clear and cold and I started walking quickly to warm up. Our apartment was in a residential neighborhood, and the houses exuded an air of safety and warmth and comfort, creating the impression of a world as it should be with everything in its proper place. That suburban world made me think I was looking at another planet, and I didn't feel connected to it, and it held no interest for me. I had no desire to be living in one of those houses, and I felt like a stranger to that world and in that moment those houses looked like prisons to me. Not my cup of tea, not what I want from life. I couldn't imagine what those people were doing there, day after day, living in such an orderly way. Something was stirring in me, a reaction to the whiskey bottle and the knife. I had a feeling that something else is needed in the world besides people living in these nice houses, and that my calling, I was surprised to hear David's word come to mind, was in a different direction.

After walking a bit, I looked up at the night sky and found the Big Dipper. It's still there - nothing is different - even though I did almost get killed. The stars were twinkling brighter than usual. I figured it was because of the cold. Eugene was having an unusually cold winter. The longer I walked, the happier I felt about still being alive and unharmed. Once again, I had escaped from danger, unharmed. I had survived Lance and his whiskey bottle and knife. No doubt about it, it had been a close call, and while I could take no credit for Lance's dramatic change in mood from psycho killer to pathetic crybaby, I did feel good about my refusing to drink with him. A new wave of determination came over me. I looked up again at the sky.

"God," I said, and immediately regretted being so silly as to think God was up in the sky.

I looked at the ground and repeated myself, "God, wherever you are, what is the point of all this? What is the point of this outrageous creation if it produces tormented human beings like Lance Miller? I want to know! With your help of course, but that will be my life work - to find out what is the point of all this."

I felt excited. Talking to God was not something I did or thought about doing. I wouldn't call what came out of my head praying,; it was more of a sustained and determined pep talk to myself.

My rant continued. "Not for me will be the mundane pursuit of material wealth so I can end up on a street like this one. I will seek in a new direction - inside - the universe within will be my focus, my university. I will pursue the purpose of life, the reason behind the illusion of all these temporary safe dwellings. But, first and foremost I need to get out of the prison of my thought-filled head. And God, or whatever and wherever you are, you will help me because why else did you create me if not to find my way out of this hell hole we humans are stuck in? Yes, it's obvious that Lance is living a pointless, meaningless, tortured life, and since I am subject to the same kind of thoughts and feelings and weirdness, what is keeping me from becoming like him?"

I knew nothing was keeping me from becoming like him, that there were no guarantees. It was up to me to actively pursue an answer, a way out of the labyrinth of my thought-filled head.

Justin ended a meeting in December by saying he would be starting a separate group, after the holidays, for those interested in pursuing more deeply the subjects we'd been discussing.

Finally!, I thought. I was very glad to hear him make this announcement, it was exactly what I had been hoping for.

So after the meeting I told him I was interested; however, I did wonder who would be in the group since I had not noticed new people coming. The Tuesday night meetings were usually a small group, less than fifteen, which I liked because it made it easier to participate. I had gotten to know a number of people by name, and I surmised that many of them - the regulars - were already in a group together.

From everything Justin had been saying, working on oneself by oneself was an almost pointless endeavor, doomed because an individual needs help from others to be aware moment to moment. It made sense to me that a sleeping person could not wake up without other people and according to the book, *In Search of the Miraculous,* for a group of people to wake up, they need a teacher who is awake. Which also made sense to me. But was Justin someone who was awake? He had not made that claim. When people questioned him about his qualifications as a teacher, he claimed nothing other than an ability to help someone see what they needed to do to make their next step.

Marty and Douglas were going home to visit Marty's parents in Spokane. They asked me to come around and feed their cat and watch over things while they were gone, and as thanks, Marty invited me over for a holiday dinner. She also invited David and Charles but Charles was unable to come. He had a new woman friend, and he was making hints that he'd like me to find another place to live. He wanted that apartment for himself and his new girlfriend. And as it turned out, Douglas was feeling under the weather, so it was Marty, David, and me.

During dinner we'd mainly talked about Marty's schoolwork which would be finishing up that spring. She was debating whether to go on to grad school right away, or take some time off and travel. As motivated as she was to become a real therapist, I figured she would move right on into grad school.

At a lull in the conversation David asked me, "John, you know that book you told me about, *Be Here Now*? I have read a lot of it and I'm wondering what do you think about gurus? Do you believe a guru has those powers, like to read your mind, and know what you should do with your life?"

I shrugged my shoulders, as if to say, who knows?

Marty said to me, "I know how you would have answered that. Remember your favorite album that you used to listen to all the time?"

I nodded my head slowly. "Oh yeah, I forgot about that. John Lennon, 'I Found Out.'"

"I found out? I found what out?" David asked.

"Well, 'I Found Out' is the title of the song. Basically, Lennon found out that it's all bullshit. All this stuff about gurus having magical powers. No one can help you but yourself. One of the verses goes, uh ... wait a minute."

For a moment the lyrics escaped me, it had been so long since I'd thought of this song.

Then, it all came back to me. "Oh yeah, *'Old Hare Krish, got nothing on you, just people crazy with nothing to do, keep you occupied with pie in the sky, there ain't no guru who can see through your eye.'I! I found out!*"

I was getting into singing that song, which oddly enough I had not listened to or even thought about since I had been living at 518.

"Oh my, now that's not very inspiring!" David said. He looked concerned.

"Yeah? Doesn't it depend on what you mean by inspiring? Certainly not inspiring if you want someone to believe in God and all that stuff, but how about if you want someone to take responsibility for themselves and not spend their time chasing after someone who can enlighten them by whacking them on the head?"

David still looked concerned; he was frowning, trying to figure it all out.

Marty got misty eyed. "I loved those times at 518. We had such great talks, you, Alan, me." Her voice trailed off.

I did not remember those times as fondly as she did but did not say anything. I knew it was because of how I had been at that time, confused and not knowing what direction my life should go in, and had nothing to do with her or anyone else.

I'd also had a change in my thinking. I realized I was arguing something I had no real interest in arguing. I wanted to cancel out everything I had said because in fact, I no longer thought like that.

"Well, wait, I don't believe or not believe in the words of the song. With music it's the music that makes a song great, ya know? The words are fun to sing, but does John Lennon know any more than any of us?"

Marty was aghast and almost shouted, "Oh ho, now you wait just a minute. We had a long talk about that, more than one long talk, don't you remember?"

She was sounding hurt and upset. "And you certainly did believe John Lennon was right!"

I was surprised and felt stupid when I realized that of course she was right.

"Yeah, okay, you're right. I did believe at that time that he was right. I mean of course I remember the good times we had talking, but I'd forgotten about the content of the talks. And yes, of course, I did relate to those words, but ... well, all I can say I guess is that I no longer believe in the words of that song. And at this moment it seems absurd for me to think that I ever claimed to know anything for certain. Because I don't know. I ... have not found out! So if then I claimed to know for certain that there was no such thing as a guru, then, all I can say is, I now think differently."

David asked slowly, "So, you now do believe in gurus?"

I felt like I was being put on the spot and squirmed in my seat. I wished I could speak clearly, but a pre-req for speaking clearly is thinking clearly.

"Okay, let me try to explain exactly what I do think, as of right now. I don't believe, and I don't *not* believe."

"Cop out!" shouted David. "Not allowed. Take a stand, be a man!"

Marty shouted, "Oh, my God, you didn't just say that did you? Be a *man?!*"

David was quick to backpedal on that one. "Sorry, sorry, I didn't mean that as an affront to you, as a woman. It's an expression."

Marty lifted her fist in a threatening way. "And I hate those expressions!"

David grimaced. "Marty, all I can say is, I'm sorry. Okay? Anyway, but seriously, John, you can't say yes and no at the same time. You have to choose."

I started over. "Okay, so it does sound to me, now, that meeting someone like a guru would make everything a lot easier, and so it would be nice if that were the case. Which means I am leaning towards believing in the possibility."

"Define the 'everything a lot easier.' What's the everything?"

"Uh ... well, that's the million dollar question. Enlightenment? But let me finish first before we get into what that is. The other side of the coin or possibility is that I also think there's a good chance it's all just wishful thinking. Something sounds off about it, I mean, you just get zapped and you are changed forever? Like Paul on the road to Damascus. He's going along hating Christians and even killing them, and then God zaps him and he becomes a saint. Isn't there something ridiculous about that? He didn't have to actually do anything!"

David said, "I agree with you completely! However, I do also believe that anything is possible, with God, anything is possible. So, tell me what do you mean by that word, enlightened?"

I felt frustrated and shrugged my shoulders. I had no idea what it meant, and yet, here we were throwing around these words like we knew what we were talking about.

David said, "Well, let me ask you, would an enlightened person be special in some way, would you be able to tell they are enlightened?"

"No, I don't think you'd necessarily be able to tell if someone walking down the street was enlightened."

He nodded, "Okay, so would an enlightened person be happy all the time?"

I shrugged, "Happy?" I thought about that and said, "Well, first, I think we have to define the word happy!"

"Wait, maybe that's not a good word. How about this as a question, would they ever suffer, would they ever get upset about things?"

"Uh, no. An enlightened person, in my opinion, would not ever get upset about anything, they'd be beyond that, like getting angry and pissed off and worried, none of that."

"Okay, that's good. I get that. So, would they be in a state of feeling god's presence all the time?"

That sounded good. "Yes, they would, so they'd be way beyond happy, they'd be more like ecstatic all the time. Of course, I guess it depends on how you define, 'feeling god's presence'."

"I get it, I think I know what you mean by enlightened. Let me ask you this, have you ever met anyone who is enlightened?"

"No, I have not."

David looked hurt. "What about me?"

I said, "Look, I want to go on to another point. Have you ever heard of the Fourth Way?"

"I have," Marty said. "That was in that book that Annie was into."

"Right," I said, "Annie was the one to turn me on to that book."

"What book?" David asked.

"*In Search of the Miraculous.* It describes meeting a teacher who teaches a method he calls the Fourth Way."

"So if there's a Fourth Way, there must be three ways before that?"

Marty said, "I know because I liked that book a lot. Yes, there are three ways, three traditional ways. The way of the monk. Like, David, what you are considering. That's one path. By the way, are you still considering that?"

David's head bobbed up and down in an ambivalent movement. "Uh, okay, now I'm gonna cheat and say I don't wanna talk about it. Some other time maybe, but not now."

For some bizarre reason I was disappointed to hear that he was maybe not so gung ho anymore. Marty went on.

"Then there is the path of the yogi. And the path of the fakir. They basically cover the mind, emotions, and body. The fakir learns how to control the body so he can walk on burning coals and stuff like that, and supposedly through gaining mastery of the body he can reach another level of consciousness, become enlightened. I'm not sure if the monk or the yogi is the mind or emotions. John, do you know?"

I thought I should know and realized I was not sure either. "I ... am not sure! But by following those paths, then one can also have a chance to reach another level of consciousness, or enlightenment."

David was frowning, "Okay, so what is the Fourth Way?"

"The Fourth Way is a way of awareness. By being aware in each moment then one can become enlightened."

I knew that wasn't how the mysterious teacher G had defined it in the book, but it was all I could come up with.

Marty then said, "Annie and I used to talk about this very thing. She claimed it was more a path of working on yourself, like, what was that phrase used in the book? Remembering! That was it. Remembering yourself."

David was surprised by this. "What does that mean? Remembering yourself?"

"Yes," I said, "I should have said, that's the essence of the Fourth Way path. You *remember* yourself. Which means awareness of yourself."

"That's so vague. We'd have to define awareness in each moment. I think I already am aware in each moment, and I think you are too. And you too Marty."

"Gee thanks, David."

He was sounding very sure of himself, "Some moments more than others maybe, but in each moment of life there has to be some awareness of being alive."

I said, "Yeah, but if you actually try to prove to yourself that you can remember yourself, that is, be aware of yourself during the day as you do things, then you won't be so quick to claim that you can do it!"

"But what does that mean?"

Marty said, "Annie and I had so many talks about this. She said it was like a second awareness you would have about what you were doing, or while you are doing it, you are aware of seeing yourself, like from up above your head. That was how she tried to do it. She tried to see herself doing stuff from like up there somewhere."

She got up to demonstrate, putting her hands up above her head.

This was making me nostalgic for Annie. Also, regretful that I did not have these kinds of conversations with her. I had no idea she had been so into this kind of thing.

David said, "That sounds impossible! How would you be able to actually *do* something? I mean, if you have to also be watching yourself do it?"

Marty said, "Don't ask me!"

I said, "I agree that it sounds impossible, but we're just the messengers here, telling you that is the Fourth Way."

He said, "Okay, well, let's change the subject. I want to ask you something about Ram Dass in that book *Be Here Now*. I think his book is simplistic, dangerously simplistic. Things are not as simple as Ram Dass makes them out to be. I don't believe it's that simple, that just by being here now, that one can then be 'enlightened.' And by the way, do you think that's what he meant by being here now?"

I said, "I don't think so. I mean, I think he just means basically do one thing at a time, ya know? Look, I am not an expert on any of this. I'm just beginning to explore it. Those meetings I've told you about on Tuesday nights are about the Fourth Way."

"Is that guy, Justin, that you've told me about, is he a Fourth Way teacher?"

The way David asked made it sound like Justin should be able to prove that he had the official title, *A Fourth Way Teacher.* I thought David was combining the rules of Academia with the spiritual path, which struck me as somehow not appropriate.

"I really don't know. Seems like he is. I mean he seems to know a lot about it. He doesn't really claim to be anything."

David frowned and said in a sing-song way. "I don't like that, I'm getting a bad feeling about this."

I was trying to think of something to explain why I didn't need to know Justin's credentials.

David went on, "Jesus claimed to be the way, the truth, and the life. He was quite clear and definite about who he was."

"Why are you bringing up Jesus? What's Jesus have to do with this? I'm not into Jesus, I don't care what Jesus …"

David held his hands up to signal me to back off and Marty interrupted, "Hey, John, calm down. Let's not get carried away with this!"

I shut up realizing that yes, I was pissed off, and I was not sure why, but I wanted to defend Justin

David said, "But don't you think a teacher, of anything, should know their abilities and what they know or don't know and should make them clear to those people who are willing to become students? When I started my class I made it clear what kind of teacher I was, that I was there to learn from the students …"

He droned on while I was trying to get my emotions under control.

When he finished, I said, "Look, here's the thing. It's in his style of teaching that makes me want to come back and hear more. So, the proof is in the pudding, not in what credentials he has. From the things he says and the way he responds to people, they are evidence of something, and that something is indefinable, it's mysterious, but the end result is that it inspires confidence in me for him and what he is teaching."

David took this in, but asked, "What does he charge?"

"Nothing, so far anyway, it's free, no money involved. And you know I just thought of a good example. I took piano lessons on the east coast from a guy who was very well known in the D.C. area, where I grew up. But I never knew about his fame and credentials when I started taking lessons from him. All I knew was that I really liked his lessons, and that I was really inspired after the lesson to go home and practice. It wasn't the diplomas or credentials hanging on the wall that inspired me, which he didn't have hanging on the wall anyway. His actual teaching in the lessons is what made me want to come back. It wasn't until later on that I found out he was actually well known and had this reputation as being a great teacher."

I didn't want to insult David so I didn't tell him that his classes on Martin Buber, while they were fun and interesting, did not hold a candle to Justin's meetings. And the reason had nothing to do with diplomas or credentials, or with David's speeches to the students about how much he wanted everyone to learn from each other. It had to do with Justin's ability, in any given moment, to provide clarity by directing a discussion into an unexpected direction.

Chapter 7

Bo asked me to drive him to the airport. He was going back east to visit his family, and he said I could use his car, a latest model pretty blue Audi, while he was gone if I agreed to take him to the airport and pick him up when he returned. I wondered how, or if, my life would change having a car to use since my mode of transportation had been foot, hitchhiking, and a cheap bike I had bought at a yard sale. Since we were in the middle of Eugene's rainy season that car looked very good.

His flight was late at night, so he came over and we talked together till it was time to take him to the airport. I had not seen much of Bo the last few weeks as he had been very busy with end of term papers and exams.

"Where's Anna?"

"San Francisco. To see her family."

"I thought she was from New York City?"

"Yeah, she is, but they wanted to meet her in San Fran. Have you ever been?"

"Oh yeah. A few times. I've spent a few weekends there, not much though. It's cold, that's my impression of that city. It's cold and windy."

"Well yeah. That's what Candlestick is famous for. Juan Marichal getting blown off the mound when he does his big kick wind up."

Marichal was the star pitcher for the S.F. baseball team. Bo got up to demonstrate and did a pretty good job of it, but pitching windups were my specialty. Ever since I'd been ten years old I've loved doing the pitcher's wind up. I got up and demonstrated but of course Bo would not admit mine was any better than his. Then he got into pretending he was the batter stepping into and out of the batter's box. I could tell he had dreamed of being a big league batter the way he went through the motions.

"How are you and Anna doing? Anything happening there of interest?"

Bo grimaced. His body started doing a herky-jerky dance as he got ready for my next 100+ mph fastball.

"It's impossible for me to determine what is happening in her head. I don't know if she sees me as an interesting experiment or she's using me for my knowledge of film…"

I completed a huge windup, delivering a fastball to Bo, and he swung and then lifted his arm as if he was watching it leave the ballpark. Then he started trotting around the room, as if he was circling the bases, and making the roar of the crowd sound with his open mouth.

I hung my head in mock anguish.

He shouted, "Oh yeah, there's something I gotta show you. Here, look at this."

He forgot about being a batter and he turned into a self-righteous angry young man. With a classic Bo disgusted look, he threw something at me. I picked it up, it was his film paper. On the front of it was a big fat red A with a circle around it and a note that said, "Excellent job, as usual Robert. See you next term in the seminar."

"I don't get it, what's the problem? You got an A!"

"Yeah, yeah, I know, but get this, man, Anna got an A+ with a whole page of notes from him. I got nothing but that note on the front. There's nothing to indicate he even read it. I bet he didn't! And, the thing is, I helped her with her paper. In fact, I gave her her thesis. It was *my* fucking idea!"

"Jeez, Bo, come on, this seems like extreme paranoia or something. Appreciate what you got! And anyway, a thesis is one thing, but being able to write well enough to get an A+ means she did the work, right?"

"No, no, you're not getting it. I *helped her* with the writing. I helped her *organize* it."

"Okay, well ..." I was searching for the silver lining in this, "So that means you must have spent quite a bit of time with her."

"Yeah, I did, and you know why, but there was no pay-off. You know? Nothing. And, I don't know, I'll do anything and maybe that's my problem. I'm fucking desperate. I haven't been laid all semester. I have no problem helping her to get an A+ if, and it's a big if, we become lovers. Tell me, what do you think of her? Give me your assessment."

And then he shouted out as an afterthought, "And my chances, what do you think my chances are? Don't pussyfoot around Kreilkamp, gimme the straight dope."

I sighed. I had been enjoying doing the windup and being in my twelve-year-old's mind-set. But spending time with Bo usually meant saying stuff that I would rather not say. Especially when he put me on the spot wanting to know what his chances were with a woman.

I tried to do one more windup, but my heart was no longer into it. I sat down.

"Let's see. First of all, Anna, I like her. A lot. I think she's really attractive. Not in a Hollywood type way, but in an interesting way. She looks like she just got off the boat from, I don't know, Romania or something? And she's obviously smart, very smart. And she knows how to talk, she's fun to talk to, she's entertaining, she knows what she wants, she's serious, she's maybe the most serious person I've met in a long time."

Bo was nodding his head, agreeing with my compliments of the woman he was interested in.

"A huge improvement on Charlotte, that's for sure. But does she have any interest in you?"

He said, "Look, I know she's using me. That's my gut feeling about it. I hate to say it, but the fact is, I would rather be used by her and hang on to my slim chance than *not* be used by her, that's how desperate I am. But I don't know if she's just a total tease or what. What do you think? I mean, like, about me? Have you ever talked to her, I mean, alone, without me there?"

"No, I never have. Never seen her, never had the chance. What does she do, where does she hang out?"

"She doesn't hang out. At least, I don't think she does, unless she's lying to me. But she gets fucking straight A's. She is more of a fanatic about grades than I am. She is fucking majoring in Russian with another major in Eastern European Lit. She seems to spend all her time doing schoolwork. So, look, here's the thing, she will be back in Eugene in a few days, before I get back. Why don't you try to talk to her to find out what's going on with her, I mean, related to me of course."

Bo was suddenly demanding me to do some undercover work for him. Not what I had been expecting, but something about this appealed to me, and at the same time I knew something was off about it but didn't know what exactly.

"I don't know, I mean I never run into her, so it's unlikely I'll see her."

He said, "Got it covered, here's her phone number. I want you to give her something for me, that will you give you an excuse to meet her."

Bo had this crazy scheme all figured out.

"Ah, wow, okay, uh, so what exactly do you want me to find out? What her feelings are for you? That's it?"

"Yeah, that pretty much covers it. That's what I want to know. Just talk to her, nice and casually of course, and see if something interesting comes out. Like, does she have a boyfriend back home maybe?

Is she a lesbian? Spend a little time with her and observe, and tell me what you think."

"We'll see, Bo, I don't know if her sexual desire for men or women will come up in a conversation with her, but I guess I'm willing to try. What is it you want me to give to her?"

"This." He picked up the album he had brought with him. "I want her to hear this guy. Skip James. He wrote the song 'I'm So Glad.' In fact, I want you to hear it, right now."

"The song Cream did?"

"Yeah, man, Cream did it also, Cream covered it, but Skip James wrote it, and his version is so fine, so fine. Dig it, the guy lived most of his life in absolute obscurity. He died a few years ago, but this is an outrageous version of 'I'm So Glad,' you gotta hear it.

He put it on. It was an outrageous version. And we each got lost in our own world of pretending to be a blues singer.

So there I was in Eugene over Christmas with most of my friends gone, but I had an outrageous car to drive around in. My mother sent me a gift package filled with the treats she baked. Which I then proceeded to eat over the next two days, which meant my stomach was in an uproar for the next week from all those rich goodies.

This was to be my last week in the apartment as I had agreed to move out. Charles and I had little in common anymore as he was immersed in his photography studies, and he had no curiosity in what I was doing, searching for a greater meaning to life than could be found in art. I admired Charles for trying to be an artist. Just like I admired Alonzo for his pursuit of so many different things. For them, their interest had consumed their lives, and Charles could not figure out why, after giving several years of my life to the piano, I was now giving up. I didn't think I was giving up. I was still practicing the piano, but I knew what he meant. My priority had shifted. I was no longer putting all my eggs into the music basket. I definitely was not going for music the way I had been or the way he was going after photography.

I found a cheap room to rent in a very large old house that had been converted into rental rooms. It had a huge kitchen that we all shared. Tom, an older guy I had met at Justin's meetings, lived there and had told me there was a room opening up. It was across from campus and within one block of the music building, which is where I went to practice the piano, so I thought it would be a great place to live.

I was wrong about that, but it certainly proved to be interesting.

I called Anna later in the week and arranged to meet her at the Odyssey Café one evening. As I waited for her I wondered how to go about getting information out of her. She showed up late and came over to my table but did not sit down.

"Hi, how are you, you have something from Robert?"

I was not prepared for her being all business like this. I'd figured she'd at least sit down. And I didn't want to just give her the record and have her walk away, nothing would have been accomplished.

Stalling, I said, "Yeah, yeah, you want a cup of tea?"

"Oh, no, I'm busy, I've got some people I need to meet."

"Okay, well, here it is, what Bo wants you to listen to." I picked up the album and gave it to her. "Bo - Robert - really wants you to listen to the song, 'I'm So Glad.' Do you like blues?"

She shrugged her shoulders. "Am I supposed to? I don't know, maybe. I'm not a huge fan, but Robert has been trying to open my mind up to it. Maybe this will help. Okay, so, thanks. See you around."

She started to walk away, somewhat hesitatingly. I said, "Oh, wait." I was determined to not have her walk away but had no idea what to say. She turned and I blurted out, "Hey, why don't we listen to it together?"

She smiled and said, "Sure, that sounds great. You could come over to my place in about an hour, I'll be free then." And then she gave me her address.

Exciting! So, I would get a chance to talk to Anna, the great intellectual. I would probe the depths of her mind and discover the true feelings she harbored in the depths of her soul for her dear colleague and friend, Robert. Those feelings which I strongly suspected were not of the sexual nature.

But I suddenly became very nervous about this meeting with her. My suggestion that we listen to the record together could be easily misinterpreted. In my mind was the uneasy thought that Bo had told me he had never been to her apartment.

However, an hour later I was in her apartment. She was alone as her roommate had gone home for Christmas break.

After we sat down, at opposite ends of a pretty big couch, she threw me a curve ball, "I'm really curious about those meetings you go to. Are you still going?"

"Yes, I am." I was tempted to immediately tell her about Justin's talk of starting a new group, but refrained. Since she had never been to a meeting, it certainly would have been jumping the gun to try and sell her on joining a new study group.

I asked her, "Okay, so, I want to ask you, if you're curious, why haven't you come to a meeting?"

"I had a class on Tuesday night, so I couldn't come. You know that book you mentioned by Ouspensky?" She reached over and picked it up from a bookshelf. "I bought it and I've started reading it. It's quite fascinating."

From her bookmark I could see that she'd read quite a bit of it. I asked her, "What do you find fascinating about it?"

"Oh, the whole story, you know? The strange teacher G, the war, the Russian revolution, I'm majoring in Russian so it's interesting from that perspective. But what I am really intrigued by is the idea that we can access higher energies. It makes sense to me, and that's something I could really use. I have a lot I want to do, a lot I want to accomplish, I have big dreams, and so I'd like to make use of those energies. If they are in us somewhere. I mean, it drives me crazy that I waste so much time sleeping."

I nodded my head agreeing with her. I also had the idea that being able to remember myself and become more conscious would mean I would need less sleep.

She asked, "Do you guys talk about that in those meetings you go to?"

"Uh, a little, but not really, not how to access higher energies. It's more about where we're at now, ya know? What do you think about the idea of remembering yourself?"

She shrugged her shoulders. "I don't know. I don't really know what that means. What does that mean? Do you know?"

"I don't really know. But I think it's interesting to try to have an awareness of what I am doing, while I am doing it."

"But, come on, I feel like I am aware of myself and what I am doing."

"You do? Really?" I am sure I sounded incredulous, and she then immediately sounded defensive.

"Look, I get straight A's. I'm not bragging, what I'm saying is to get straight A's takes awareness. How could I have not been aware of what I was doing and gotten A's?"

I was sorely tempted to ask her a direct question about how much Bo had helped her get that A+ on the film paper, but I held myself in check.

I really didn't want to engage in an argument with her related to these ideas. She was a female version of Bo, wanting to put forth her view and then hear my view and then argue it out, either prove she is right, or hear a stronger argument to the contrary. Which I knew I would not be able to provide. I felt inadequate, like, I was clearly not in any position to be convincing someone of anything. These ideas were all still too new to me.

I said, "What you say about wanting to access higher energies reminds me. I met some people once who did Buddhist chanting for specific things, like money, or a new car, or good grades, or you know, some specific material object. And I never knew of course, were they really telling the truth? Does it really work? But this one woman I met, I could swear she was telling the truth when she described stuff she'd gotten from chanting."

Anna frowned. "So what are you saying? I should start chanting?"

"Maybe. If it's something specific you want. Like, being able to get more done."

"So why are *you* doing this, why are you going to those meetings, why are you reading books like this? What is it that you want?"

I was impressed by her genuine interest. She really wanted to know. I took a deep breath and decided to start at the beginning. I told her about my nighttime experiences - which had decreased - they now only occurred about once a month. And my wanting to find out what it was inside my head that was able to either create those outrageous experiences, or access them, or receive them. And that I didn't want to put anything before that search because I knew that if I went back to school then that would be all I'd have time for.

When I was done, she got up and went to a drawer and came back with a joint. She lit it up and passed it to me. I hesitated and then took it, remembering the poker phrase, in for a nickel, in for a dollar.

She said, "You know, I have to admit what you're saying makes some sense. I am too busy really to do anything other than school work." She took another hit and we passed it back and forth a few times.

I could feel myself getting high. It had been a few months since I had smoked and I was feeling my old nervous paranoia coming onto me.

She went on, "But, I mean, how are you gonna make a living if you don't have an education? Isn't that also important? And G says something like that in the book, to be successful in the work you have to be successful in life."

I nodded. "I know, and I don't know what to say about that. Other than, I don't want to wait to take care of this. It seems more important to me than figuring out how to make money. I can figure that out later."

Anna then happened to bring up Bo, "Oh, by the way, don't mention to Robert that I am reading this book, I really don't want to have to deal with his cynicism about it."

"Okay." I said. I then realized this gave me an opening, "So, what's going on with you and Robert?"

She said, surprised. "Me and Robert? What do you mean?"

"Well, you know, are you romantically interested in him, as more than a friend?"

"Oh, good Lord, no! He's a good friend, that's all." She smiled at me and I realized I was now in trouble. I knew I couldn't say that the only reason I had asked is because Robert wanted me to find out. So now it looked like I was asking because I was interested in her. And it that moment I realized why I'd had such a bad feeling about this whole caper.

And what was even more strange to me was that I was not interested in her, as attractive and interesting as she was. And it not certainly not because I felt some moral obligation to Bo. It was more like I had no sex drive anymore.

But she didn't know that of course, and I hardly knew it myself, but it was clear to me in this moment that I did not want the complication of being involved with Anna, nor did I physically feel any attraction for her, and yet I felt I had to go along with this.

"If you are concerned about Robert, you can relax." She moved closer. "I'm a free woman."

We started to kiss, but my heart and mind were not into it. I tried, I really tried to relax and get into the kissing but my mind would not let me, it was totally out of control. She could feel it, and she backed away.

"You alright? What's going on?"

I said, "Look, I find you really attractive and really cool, but ... I don't know, I'm just not able to ..." And my voice trailed off. I was very disappointed in myself, it was so painful to not be into what should be a great experience.

As I was walking home, my mind felt like it was in a psychic earthquake. I was disturbed and shaken up by my inability to perform. A door had been slammed shut in my face. Keep out! Not for you! Go elsewhere!

"What the fuck is wrong with me?" I wondered. On one level I just felt embarrassed, and dreaded seeing her again, but more than that was a feeling of being a loser. That night I could not fall asleep; my mind tormented me with my inadequacies.

PART TWO

FINDING

Chapter 8

With the new year came a new set of circumstances, and a renewed eagerness to keep going further on the path that seemed to be opening on its own in front of me. I had come out to Eugene searching, and I was finding. I would be in a study group led by Justin, which I was eagerly looking forward to. I would no longer be going to David's class. The *Film as Lit* class was not happening this semester, and I was about to turn 22.

Oh, and any vague fantasies I'd had about finding a girl friend had been destroyed by my experience with Anna. And I am quite certain it was sour grapes on my part, but I did convince myself that it was all for the best that I was now *not* Anna's lover.

The time came for our group's first meeting. We were to meet at an apartment in town near where I lived, and I was surprised to see that there were seven of us, most of whom I had not seen at the Tuesday night meetings.

We sat on the floor in a circle, and went around and gave our names. There was Mona, Dan, Tom, Rick, Rob, and Debbie. All of us were about the same age, except for Tom who looked to be in his thirties. Justin then talked about his philosophy around study groups.

"We call this a study group because we are studying something, and what we are studying is ourselves. You are studying you. Dan is studying Dan, Mona is studying Mona. Each of you is studying your own self. Now, that does not mean you will not get to know each other, and that does not mean you should not be paying attention to each other, but, for now, that is really secondary to the main purpose of this work which is for you to get to know you.

"You are the one who is in whatever state of awareness and consciousness you are in. For that to change there's two possibilities. Either you meet someone, like a guru, who can knock you over the head and enlighten you, or you work on yourself. You either wait for a stroke of great luck or you take the necessary steps to get yourself from where you are now to someplace higher, finer, and more real.

"Now, I also believe we need more help than we think we need in the area of getting to know ourselves. Most of us assume that whatever we need we can get by talking about it, or reading a book. But my view is we need lots of help and help of a very practical nature, and this help is similar to the help we need in doing anything. If we are going to do anything practical in this world, like grow food, build shelters, make clothes - we use tools. Hammers, knives, pots and pans, shovels. I mean, would you even think of digging a hole without a shovel? No way! And yet we think we can become more aware by just ... what? Dreaming about it? Talking about it, thinking about it, reading about it?

"Spiritual tools can help us. I would not be sitting here in front of you now, if not for my using tools. So, I will introduce tools to you, slowly, one at a time and you will experiment with using them, finding out for yourself what they can do for you, how they can illuminate certain parts of yourself to you. So, your field of study is you, and your job will be to use the tools. Not talk about them, but use them. Here in these meetings we will talk about them, so all the talking will be covered here. If you are with someone from the group, and I encourage you guys to get together, then you don't get together to *talk* about the tools. You get together to use the tools, keep the talking and discussion to a minimum. Any questions so far?"

Mona asked, "So, Dan and I are married, we have a child, what about our situation?"

Justin said, "Well, you have to be practical about it. In your case, you obviously have many interactions that will not involve tool use, but you still should have the rule of not talking about the tools with each other. You can at least follow that guideline. And of course use the situation to an advantage. You can use each other as reminders to use the tools."

Tom, the guy I knew pretty well because we were now living in the same house, asked, "How did you learn the tools? Did you have a teacher?"

Justin said, "I cannot tell you at this time about how I learned the tools. At some point, if we know each other long enough, I'm sure we will eventually get to that, but for now, it is not helpful to you to know that." He looked around for more questions while Tom grumbled about the non-answer he had received.

This much I was learning: Tom usually found something to complain about, and Justin was secretive about his past.

Justin went on, "Now, that said, tools are not the only thing we will discuss and do. I want us to read a book together. We will start with reading one chapter today. I will pass it around and each person read a page or two." He held up the book and said, "This book is called *Mount Analogue* and it is written by a man named Rene Daumal."

I had never heard of the book or the author. We read the first chapter, which certainly got all my attention. It was well written and an entertaining story about someone who was getting involved in what was described as an absurdly impossible quest, which of course made me think the story had something to do with what we were doing: studying ourselves, working on ourselves, trying somehow to change ourselves.

I had a strange sensation sitting there with these people I hardly knew, hearing us read this book out loud. It seemed so familiar. Not the story but the *reading out loud together.* I knew I had not done this before, other than as a little kid, when one of my parents would read to us at bedtime. And, who knows, maybe it was that memory that was flooding me with pleasant feelings, because it certainly struck me as a wonderful way to pass some time.

As we were leaving, Justin gave us an exercise to do for the week. He said, this is not really a tool, but something we can try for this coming week and see what we could learn from doing it. He told us to say, "God bless you" when we were saying good-bye to people.

I blurted out, "No way!"

He cocked his head at me with a twinkle in his eye. "I think this will be especially good for you."

So he was not joking, and my heart sank in disappointment. I did not consider the work to be religious, and the last thing I wanted was to *appear* religious. Eugene was filled with followers of Jesus, we called them Jesus freaks, and I certainly did not want to be mistaken for one of *them.*

And how could I say "God bless you" to Bo or one of my other friends? What would they think? They would totally get the wrong impression about me and what I was doing.

Well, not all friends; Alonzo would be happy to hear me say something like that.

So right away, I was filled with inner turmoil, dreading having to do such a ridiculously simple thing, and mentally going through all the encounters I might have and how each person would perceive that phrase coming out of my mouth.

The first chance I had to do the exercise was hitchhiking. I was getting out of the car and the people in the car were saying good-bye to me. I was thanking them for the ride, and I remembered to add, quite naturally I must say, "God bless you."

One of the women passengers smiled at me as if she was truly grateful to me for saying it. And then they were gone. I knew this was about as easy a way to do this exercise as possible, in fact, it was almost cheating. But even saying the words to total strangers who were driving away gave me a glimpse into the workings of my personality. A part of me popped up and wanted to know their reactions, what they thought of me. Another part wanted to add a disclaimer, and another part ... was really happy!

It was like an invigorating strong wind, which started blowing through me, filling me with hope and optimism. Basically the feeling was that I am not limited by my own ideas about who I am. I am not my personality! I am no longer a person who does not and cannot say, *God bless you.* I had done it! In the lamest way possible, true, but still, saying those three words gave me a way to halt the flow of my normal behavior. The ruling part of me was dethroned in that moment, that one tiny moment. I wanted to do it again and again, but of course this kind of specific exercise loses its impact after it has been done a few times.

And yes, I did try saying it with one of my friends, and though I was trying to say it sincerely, I failed. I injected a sense of drama into it; to deflect the impact of the words, I made it into a joke. And he responded in a joking manner of his own. I felt stupid, and I was humbled by the power of my personality to corrupt my intentions. My personality seemed to have a life or energy of its own. It projected itself into the world whether I wanted to or not.

And another point about this exercise or any exercise is that it is has no value in and of itself. For another person in the group, like Mona, this exercise was almost pointless since she had no problem at all saying those three words.

At another meeting Justin gave us the exercise to say no to someone when you normally would say yes. Predictably, as with most of the exercises he gave, I thought of all kinds of reasons why it was not a good exercise.
Why am I doing something that is not nice?
Does inner work require that we become anti-social?
Why would I do something to purposely hurt another?
Does working on myself mean I have to be an asshole?
At that time I was renting a room in a huge house just off-campus. There must have been twenty other people renting rooms in this old Victorian mansion, and I was on friendly terms with some of them by virtue of our living together, sharing a kitchen and central living space.
The rooms were cheap to rent, and I found out there was a reason for that. I could tell a number of stories about the strange characters living in this house, but I think that would detract from this story I am telling.
One evening I ate dinner with Brian, a thin, nervous guy who seemed to be on the verge of laughing hysterically about something, or flying out the window. After we had finished eating, I got up to leave. He asked me where I was going. I said to a certain bookstore nearby.
He said, "Oh, I've been meaning to go to that bookstore, okay if I tag along?"
He rose out of his chair as he asked it, assuming in his mind that his question was rhetorical, and that I would say yes.
And here it was, a perfect opportunity to say no when I would normally feel obliged to say yes,

because in fact, I certainly did not want to walk to the bookstore with him. Eating dinner with him for twenty minutes was as much as I could handle.

I said no.

He was stunned and looked like a wounded animal, really hurt; he was crushed. I was dismayed by his reaction, but knew there was nothing I could say that would make any sense to him. I could not ease the pain, the discomfort in either him or myself.

I watched myself writhing inside trying to make it okay in my head for the cruel thing I had just inflicted on this poor defenseless guy. While one part of me felt terrible about saying no to Brian, there was also that part of me which was overjoyed that I'd said no to him. It congratulated me for finally speaking the truth because normally I would not have had the guts to say no.

I ran into Alonzo one day. I had not seen much of him in the past few months. He was very excited about the new place he had found to live. It had a piano, and he wanted me to come over and try it out. And so I did. He had a plan to play music at the Odyssey Café and wanted me to play with him. So we started getting together to rehearse for our first gig. He also urged me to move in with him, there was plenty of room, and the rent would be as cheap as where I was then living. I was a little reluctant because I had lived with Alonzo before, and it had eventually gone badly.

Time passed, and I discovered some members of my group were more into making effort than others. I concluded that the group was lacking enough people who were serious about the work. More than half the members were still testing the waters, dipping a toe in and then complaining about how cold the water was. Debbie, when she was there, hardly ever spoke up. Tom was openly skeptical of the exercises and tools and was more interested in standing on the sidelines and giving his opinion instead of getting in there and mixing it up. Rick and Rob were enthusiastic and keen on discussing higher consciousness but seemed to be unable to apply themselves to doing the exercises and tools. They were avid karate practitioners and that was their passion. Mona and Dan were the only others sincerely interested in the work, and unfortunately they were the only ones who did not live in town; they lived on a commune outside of town.

Since we were not living together, the amount of time we had to actually practice the work together was limited. Sometimes the group would meet for dinner. Sometimes I would visit Dan and Mona on their commune, or I would hang out with Rick, Rob, or Tom, who all lived near me, or I would run into members of Justin's other group who I was getting to know and who also lived near me. Gradually I was spending less time with my Bo Willy circle of friends and more time with people in the work.

I decided to go ahead and move in with Alonzo. He was supportive of anything new and different, and he wanted to know all about this new group I was a part of and was not interested in arguing against it, or finding what was wrong with it.

I saw a poster at the cafe about a new class forming to teach Tai Chi, described as a moving meditation practice. That sounded right up my alley. The person teaching it was named Ismael Pentateuch, who I discovered was a beautiful tall, pregnant woman. At the first class, she did a demonstration of the movements, and I was spellbound watching her body move in slow motion.

I became an avid student and practiced daily and soon I was able to go through all the movements uninterrupted. I was convinced that whoever had created these movements was telling a story, and that the story was transmitting esoteric knowledge which could only be understood as one learned and practiced the movements and became more in tune with them. I became somewhat obsessed with trying to get something more out of the movements, the *meaning* behind them.

I practiced the Tai Chi in private but when I had learned all the movements sufficiently, I did a demonstration for Alonzo.

After I was done he said, "Wow, man, that's really great. I have an idea. I'm gonna get out my violin and play while you go through the movements."

And so he did. He played a piece that was one of his favorites, a Bach Chaconne. I found the violin music did not distract me at all, in fact, it seemed to allow me to enter into the movements more deeply.

When he stopped he said, "John, I know what we will do. We'll do this at the cafe as one of our pieces. It will be great. You'll do Tai Chi, and I will accompany you on the violin. People will dig it, I know."

"Alonzo, no way. Not at the cafe. There's too much going on there. I don't want to do …"

He shouted, "John, you cannot say no to this. This is a great idea, and you have to go along with it, seriously, man, I will not let you weasel out of this."

"Okay, okay," I said, "fine, but I need more time to practice, I'm not ready yet to do these in public with a lot of people watching, I mean, I barely know them, and also, I'm not an expert…"

He interrupted me again, "Blah, blah, blah, you're trying to get out of it! Our gig is not until next month, so you will have plenty of time to perfect your technique, and we have to practice other things too, we need at least a half hour of material, really we need an hour, but at least half an hour."

I knew that Alonzo was very good for me. If it was up to me, I would never get around to performing, but he would not stop pushing me in that direction, and strangely enough, I did not lose any sleep worrying about it. Normally this kind of event looming in my future would drive me crazy.

One weekend Justin invited us all out to his place in the country for what he referred to as a "work day." I was excited about this because we'd finally get to see where he lived and we'd also do something together, work together and try to use tools and do exercises together. In my imagination I figured this would lead somewhere different. I had no specific idea where it would lead, but I had read in books about people working together and trying to do inner work while doing specific tasks, and I was looking forward to it.

Those of us in town met up and then drove in a van to pick up Dan and Mona as they lived on the way. We had decided to use a certain tool that Justin had given us while we were in the car. It was a tool related to negative emotions and was extremely difficult, for me anyway, to put into practice with other people around. Then the car broke down. It was overheating. We pulled over to the side of the highway and all got out while Dan, who knew something about cars, looked at what was happening. It was really a perfect moment to use this tool, since all of us had to be experiencing some kind of negative emotion, and yet, none of us were able to remember that we had even set an intention to do so.

That experience made me feel a bit depressed and overwhelmed by what we were attempting. This would not be easy.

At any rate, we did arrive and Justin's place was beautiful. There was a big, friendly dog named Zup and a few horses and even sheep grazing on a large hillside pasture next to the house. Justin started by gathering us on his front lawn and giving us some guidelines for the day.

"I want you to focus on making observations. And the observations can be about anything you notice. And you say them out loud, not to yourself. What you are doing, what you see other people doing, what you are thinking, what you are feeling, what you see, maybe what you do not see. Whatever. Can be anything."

Rob asked, "Can you give an example?"

"Sure, how about this, you are all standing in a line, facing me, no one made a circle, none of you are facing out that way, or that way." And he pointed with his hand to the hillside next to the house which is where the sheep were grazing, which is naturally where we all then turned to look.

Tom said, "But that's because we are listening to you."

Mona laughed and said, "We're like those sheep, we all line up in the same way."

Justin said, "It was an example of an observation, Tom. You are hearing it as a judgment."

Tom responded quickly, "Oh, come on, it was too a judgment. Sounded like a judgment to me anyway."

Justin said, "Tom, later I might want to talk about what you are saying, but first I want you guys to practice making observations. And yes, some observations will come out of your mouths sounding like judgments, but don't worry about it. The point is to say what you are seeing, what you are noticing. And don't think each observation you make has to be profound. Please, *don't* try to make profound observations. Just make them."

I asked, "Do we talk about them after we make them?"

"No! No talking about them. Do you hear me Tom?"

Tom objected, "Why are you picking on me now? Jeez, I'm sorry for saying anything."

Justin ignored him and said, "The point is to make them, get used to saying them out loud. And start with simple, obvious ones."

The first thing we all did was load trash onto his old, yellow pickup truck. No one made any observations; then, at some point, Justin reminded us. And then we all made observations about everything.

"This is heavy."

"This is not heavy."

"This is disgusting."

"This has a nail in it."

"The dog is watching us."

"The sun is in the sky." This got some laughs.

"We're not gonna be able to fit all of this in the truck."

I said, "Tom is picking out the lightest stuff." I knew this would get to him. He made a face at me. "Tom is making a funny face at me."

He had his turn. "John seems to be really full of something, hmm… I wonder what he's so full of?"

After we'd loaded as much as we could onto the truck, Justin told Dan and I to take the truck to the dump. He gave us directions - it was a few miles away, pretty simple to get there. He told Dan to drive and as we were pulling away, he called out and ran up to the window and said, "Oh, also, don't get out of first gear, so don't go faster than 15 mph."

Then he turned and was gone.

Dan was incredulous. "Huh, what does he mean?"

I laughed and said, "I think he means, don't get out of first gear, only go 15 mph."

"You gotta be fucking kidding me!"

I laughed. Suddenly, I had a wave of a feeling pass through me, which I can only describe as, "I-am-so-happy-to-be-here-this-is-fucking fantastic!"

For one thing, it was a beautiful day, and I was outside in the country. I was doing something with people that I would never have dreamed I would be doing. We were doing something normal, taking a load of trash to the dump, but we were also doing something else, on another level, paying attention to ourselves, to what was happening inside us. And the icing on the cake was Justin's last minute instruction. I thought it was perfect.

Dan had trouble with Justin's last minute command. His repeated observations were around what other drivers were thinking of us going along so slowly.

"That guy is laughing at us."

"I know that guy behind us is pissed off."

"Those people are looking at us, like what the hell is wrong with that guy."

Eventually though we were both laughing at how difficult it was to go so slowly. We purposely tried to have a normal conversation about something to get his mind off it, but that did not really work because he would then forget and start to shift into 2nd gear, and I'd have to remind him, or he would realize it himself and then curse and downshift back into 1st. One time he got all the way into third gear before we remembered. Then I decided that I would hold onto the gear shift, it was on the floor between us, and that solved that issue.

When we got back everyone was sitting under some trees having lunch, and when we were done eating Justin asked some questions about the observations we had made, what kind of observations had people heard, any observations which stood out as interesting. People said most observations were basically about what they had seen happening, like, someone picking something up, or the blackberry bushes have sharp needles, or the hill is steep, or the horses smell nice.

I told everyone that Justin had told Dan to only drive in first gear and described our difficulties in the drive to the dump and all the observations about what people must be thinking about us, like Dan saying that he was sure people were laughing at him. This got a few laughs, and Justin said that this was a good segue into the next subject he wanted to cover, which was to introduce a new tool for us to use.

"And this will also address what you called a judgment earlier, Tom. I call this tool the 'I feel that you' tool. Or, the 'I feel that he she or it' tool. In the case of Dan driving to the dump, he would have said, if he was using this tool, I feel that man is laughing at us. The terminology is important because it is stating right off the bat that you recognize that you are having a feeling about someone else, which of course is a judgment, right? *I* feel that *he* is laughing at me. I feel that he is pissed. I feel that you are bored. I feel that you are unhappy. I feel that you don't really understand me. I feel that you are a lousy cook. I am making a judgment about someone, or something, else."

He looked around at us. I understood this; it seemed pretty simple.

I said, "I feel that Mona is squirming around a lot."

She snorted and came right back with, "I feel that John has a really big mouth."

Dan said, "I have a question. Do they have to be negative?"

"No, they don't have to be negative, but, if you actually do try to use this tool, you will discover that most of the ones you have are negative. And, look, let's not get into negative or positive, it is not a helpful way to look at things anyway. What's important is to open your mouths and get these judgments out into the open, so you can hear them and so everyone around you can hear them."

Tom asked, "So, is this another tool about negative emotions?"

Justin tilted his head to the side to consider this. "Yeah, but it's more a tool to help us say out loud what is going on in our heads. Ever heard of sorting? Sorting out your feelings? This tool is a great help in doing that. Now, this tool has two parts to it. I just gave you the first part. For now, let's work on expressing them. Later on, I will give you the other part to it. So, for now, no talking about them, no discussion about it, no feeling offended because someone says, they feel you are an idiot. Okay, Rick?"

Rick looked confused. We all laughed. Rick was not an idiot, but he seemed to like to pretend he was one, at least when we were all together. I had spent some time with him alone and he was as intelligent a guy as anyone else, but for some unknown reason in the group he became stupid.

I realized I should open my mouth and say it. "I feel that Rick looks confused."

Justin went on, "And also, for now anyway, do not do this exercise with people who are not in this study group. It is definitely not a good idea to say them out loud. People will not understand."

Even though it was a fairly simple tool to understand, I soon realized it wasn't so easy to get these kind of observations out of my mouth. Doing this exercise meant telling someone, albeit indirectly, exactly what I thought of them, and something which would normally *not* be expressed. For each of the various members in the group, I had different judgments.

To Tom it would be, "I feel that you are always negative."

To Rob and Rick, "I feel that you guys are too much in love with your karate practice to be serious about what we are doing here."

To Debra, "I feel that you never have anything interesting to say."

Or, to Dan, "I feel that you are too careful."

To Mona, "I feel that you are really sexy." And that she was married with child suited me fine in my current hung-up sexual state.

And what about to myself? What judgment would I have to myself?

Probably something to do with trying to impress the teacher.

Needless to say, these were statements I found very confronting to share. And so did the others because the rest of the afternoon I only heard a few of them from the others.

At the end of the day, Justin invited us inside the house for dinner. He told Debbie and I to prepare the food with the guideline we could make whatever we wanted with what we found in the kitchen.

I had a lot of fun making the dinner with Debbie. Justin had told us to have the intention to say our judgments out loud with each other, and so we were doing that. I found out she knew about as much about cooking as I did, which was not much. So, we were both nervous when it came time to bring the food out to everyone around the table waiting hungrily for it.

I had a familiar panicky feeling as we set down the various bowls of food, wanting to assure people that it really was not any good. Then Justin told Debbie to go get a big bowl, and then he had me put all the food into it so it was all mixed up. People thought we would be disappointed, but I had the opposite reaction. The pressure was now off; since it was all mixed up together, who knows what it was supposed to taste like, and so no one could blame the cooks!

Around the dinner table we got into a discussion about careers and life work, how important a career was. Tom asked Justin how he supported himself. Justin answered that he had arrived at a place in his life that he did not have to think about money. Tom pressed him for details, and Justin said that this might sound unusual, but that each one of us could also be in this same position.

Tom was incredulous and wanted to know exactly how Justin got his money.

Justin said, "I'm not going to talk about money. But I will tell you this, that 80% of what I do, I have never done before."

I was struck by this, but then I realized that I could say the same thing about my life. Tom, the eternal doubter, did not believe it though. "How can you say that? That can't possibly be true!"

I interrupted him, "Tom, I feel that you always argue the other side of whatever is said."

Tom was quick to retort, "That's right, because none of you sheep would dare to disagree with him."

Justin said, "Say it like I instructed."

Tom looked startled, like he had no idea what Justin was talking about, and I also for a moment was caught off guard and then remembered the tool.

Tom thought a moment and said, defiantly, "I feel that you are all sheep."

Justin said, "Okay, this a good time for me to explain the second part of the tool."

He got up and went to the chalkboard, which he had hanging on the wall in the living room. He drew a stick figure with arrows pointing out from it, and then another stick figure with arrows around it pointing inward towards it.

"Both of these stick figures represent John."

Pointing at the first stick figure, he said, "I feel that you."

And then pointing at the second stick figure, the one with the arrows point inward, "And this one is I feel that I."

"John just said to Tom, 'I feel that you always disagree.'" He pointed at the stick figure with the arrows pointing away from it. "That's the first part. The second part is the 'I feel that I.' So, in this case,

John, instead of telling Tom that you think he disagrees, you say what *you* are feeling."

I was confused.

He said, "Try it. 'I feel that I …'"

"I feel that I … think that you disagree too much? No, that can't be it."

Justin said, "You need to remember what you were feeling before you put it on someone else. What were you feeling? That's what I am getting at, for you to say what *you* were feeling."

"Uh, okay." And then it was my turn to feel like an idiot. Finally, I said, "I feel that I am pissed off?"

"Yeah, okay, that's a start. You feel that you are pissed. It can be more precise though. Remember what I said about sorting? Sorting out what you are feeling? It can take a while. Tom, let's go to what you said: 'I feel that you guys are sheep.' Right? Okay, so do you want to take a crack at saying what was happening in you before you pointed it outside of you?"

Tom creased his brow in a serious frown. "Hmm … I feel that I … need to be the one to say stuff."

"Okay. That's good. Can you say it as a feeling you are having?"

"I feel that I …am smarter?" He shook his head and blew out a big breath; he was stuck. I was stuck with him, having no idea what I would say in his shoes.

Mona said, "How about this: 'I feel that I am better than you guys?'"

Tom frowned again and, nodding his head, said, "Yeah, that's true, I do feel I am better than you guys. But, how is that a feeling?"

Justin said, "Again, it can be more precise than that. Maybe feeling superior? Looking down on someone is a feeling. Remember the list of negative emotions we made? Sometimes consulting that list can help. But here's the thing. If you are pointing your finger at someone saying they are stupid or they don't speak up, or whatever, you are also having a feeling. And the work is about recognizing the feeling that you are having. That feeling is the starting point of the eventual judgment that you express onto something or someone outside of you."

We sat there for a while in silence. I was struck by two things. One, that what Justin had just said sounded very much like Truth, with a capital T. The other thing that struck me was how far I was from being aware of these kinds of feelings - being that stick figure which is aware of itself first.

Justin went on, "I cannot emphasize enough the importance of getting morality out of this. We are very hung up in this culture on right and wrong, good and bad, positive and negative. Self-knowledge is not about that. It is about impartial observation. There is no need to also have an accompanying judgment."

Chapter 9

Another exercise he gave us involved listening to music. At one of the meetings at his place in the country, he put on a record, and instructed us to hear the bass sounds in our stomach, the middle sounds in our heart and the higher sounds in our heads. The music was about 20 minutes long; it was *Bolero* by Ravel. I didn't really feel anything. He told us not to worry about whether or not we felt anything, the point was to try and hear the sounds in these different parts of our body. He told us to try this at home with music that had no lyrics, just instrumental.

I went to the library one day and checked out *Bolero* so I could listen in one of the listening booths. This time I did experience something for sure; I felt a separation between these three parts of my body as the music made me focus on the different parts.

It was vague though, and the next time I listened it did not happen.

At one meeting Justin asked us about states of consciousness, and about our experiences with other states of consciousness. We mentioned the obvious ones: marijuana, alcohol, other drugs, and also running, going out into nature, climbing a mountain - all various ways to get out of one's normal state of mind. Justin said that he wanted us to experiment with these, and that we would start with chanting, since that seemed more of a group activity that we could do pretty easily without much effort.

So one evening we gathered at Rob's apartment, but before we started chanting, Justin poured something out in cups for each of us to drink.

"What is it?," someone asked.

Justin just grinned and said, "Drink it, find out."

I thought it odd that he was not telling us what was in the drink, but I assumed it was another chance to see something about myself. I did not have trust issues with him, my instincts told me he would not do something to hurt us. And I also realized I liked the unknown element, the mystery. I picked up a cup and drank it.

Tom was not happy about this. "Wait a minute, you're not gonna tell us what's in the drink. I ain't drinking something if I don't know what it is!"

Justin ignored him. Tom was clearly pissed.

Someone piped up, "You can always say no!"

Justin said, "Okay, so, before we get started let's take a walk around the neighborhood."

We followed him outside. I felt good, excited, looking forward to what was coming but also able to relax into the beauty of the moment, walking in the half light of an early spring evening. Eugene is a pretty town, and after a winter of rain, especially so.

Dan and Justin were in front. I was behind them, and the others behind me. Dan asked a question.

"Hey Justin, I've been looking into homeopathic medicine. You know about that?"

"Some."

There was silence.

Justin said, "Dan, are you gonna say anything more about it?"

"Oh, I guess I figured you didn't want to talk about it."

"Really? Dan, relax, okay?"

"Okay, yeah, well, so we gave some to Mr. B because he had a cold and it seemed to work. He was much better today." Mr. B was their two-year-old son.

Again, silence.

Finally Dan asked, "Well, I guess I'm wondering what you think of it, if you think it works."

Justin asked, "Do you know the theory behind it?"

"Yeah, somewhat. That it's very tiny amounts of something that would be bad for you in large amounts."

"Yeah, so, what do you think of that?"

"Uh ... I don't know. I guess it makes sense, but it's such a tiny amount, supposedly, in the dose."

"Well, let me ask you, do you know what the body does with the tiny amount?"

"Uh, well, it fights it, I assume, but I'm not sure.

"I don't know enough about it either, but for the sake of this discussion, let's assume it is able to handle fighting the small amount. Can you think of anything similar to how that works?"

"Similar? Like something similar to a small amount of something that would be normally bad for you in larger amounts?" Dan was quiet as he was thinking about this. My own brain was trying to figure out what Justin was getting at, what he was comparing that too.

Finally, Justin said, "What about in the realm of what we are doing, studying ourselves?"

At this point we had gone around the block and Justin just kept on walking. I started to laugh, I had no idea why, something about his not stopping made me laugh.

Mona asked loudly from somewhere behind me, "What's so funny, John?"

I ignored her because Dan had started talking again.

He said, "I don't know, I can't think of anything."

Justin said, "Well, it might be kind of a stretch, comparing this to homeopathy, but ... what about the idea that if you take a small moment, as small a moment as you can possibly be aware of, and you start with that, then you can begin to study yourself."

Dan nodded his head, "Okay. I can see that."

Mona caught up with me. "Why didn't you answer me?"

Justin turned and looking at me said, "So, in this small moment, what's happening with you?"

I stopped literally in my tracks, and someone bumped into me from behind.

"Uh, okay, well, I was really into listening to your conversation with Dan." I could hear my voice sounding defensive which further annoyed me because I knew this was not about finding out what I did wrong and why should I feel defensive?

I started again, "I was listening to you and Dan talk, and then Mona asked me …. uh, okay, well, first I laughed because I thought about how funny it would be if we just kept walking around the block all night. I'm not sure why that is funny but anyway, that's why I laughed, but then I wanted to hear what Dan was gonna say to your question to him. So, when Mona asked me why are you laughing, I didn't think it was important, it was just some silly thought I'd had, and I really wanted to hear your conversation."

Mona said, "Why didn't you just tell me that, instead of ignoring me?"

"Because if I had taken the time to tell you that, I would have missed the conversation I was trying to listen to."

"Really? Sorry, but that's bullshit. You could easily have said that and then continued to listen."

I did not agree but was willing for the sake of stopping the argument to let her be right, "Okay, so … let's say you're right."

Mona said, "If it wasn't because you wanted to hear the conversation then why didn't you answer me?"

"So, why didn't I just answer you?" I thought for a moment. "Okay, well, I was annoyed you asked me, and I didn't want to encourage you, I think I was afraid that I'd have to explain myself more. But, uh, well, that doesn't make sense, does it. Cause if I'd just told you that I want to listen to their conversation you would have not kept talking to me."

Why hadn't I just told her the truth? I was mystified as to why I didn't just tell her the truth.

And then it hit me, I had no idea why I laughed, so, why am I making all this stuff up?

"Look, I have no idea why I laughed. Right when I laughed I didn't know why I'd laughed. So, maybe I didn't want to admit that to you, which I would have to do by answering you."

She said, "Or, another possibility. That you were afraid to find out why you had laughed."

I pondered that and thought that might very well be the case.

She kept at it, "So why do you think you laughed?"

I wanted to slug her. I had just told her that I didn't know why I had laughed. And then I realized once again I was trying to weasel out of thinking about it.

I took a deep breath and said, "Wow, let me think about that. Uh, Justin did something unexpected. I laughed, so it was almost like a nervous reaction. Could this be like on some level a physical reaction, my physical body was expecting to go one direction, and then could not, so it released this energy by laughing?"

No one said anything. Justin started us walking again.

I asked, "So laughing to me feels more like a positive emotion than a negative one. Is laughing really a negative thing we're doing, I mean like expressing a negative emotion?"

No one said anything.

Justin said, "Sounds like a great area to explore. Make some observations, pay attention to your laughter, maybe you'll learn something about it."

Then he went on, "It takes time to be able to do this. This, as small a moment as it was, may be too big. But thank Mona, John, thank her for asking you that question."

"Okay, yeah, thank you Mona."

She smiled at me. At that moment, I felt something for her that was not just a friendly feeling. I could feel myself falling in love with her. She was kind of exotic looking, like an earth mother, long blonde hair, large breasts, beautiful blue eyes.

And, along with that feeling was the awareness that she was off limits, being married with a child.

Justin continued, "I have not talked about this much yet, but since Mona asked a good question, I want to tell you that it is important to ask questions of each other. As annoying as those questions may be, that's what you have to do, you have to learn to annoy each other. Let's go inside."

We sat on the floor in a room with only candlelight. Justin started with a simple melody, singing the word *Rama* repeatedly. I got into it in a big way, as if I was leaving a major part of myself behind, or that I had been moved into a different place inside my head. And slowly it became an emotional experience for me, I was out of my head completely, and feeling something.

The chanting interrupted the normal set of interactions that took place in the group. I was no longer facing the person across the room from me in a social context that I was familiar with. I didn't know if it was my imagination or if chanting made me more sensitive to the surroundings. I could sense Tom was not into the chanting and his presence was a drag on the energy. Almost on cue, Tom abruptly got up and left. The chanting then shifted into another, higher gear.

When it was over I walked part of the way home with Mona and Dan. Mona was talking non-stop the whole way. I felt super-sensitive to what was happening. I felt that she was feeling something for me just as I was feeling something for her, and that Dan was bored and had not really experienced anything from chanting. I definitely felt high, but it was subtle, and I could not tell if it was from the chanting, or if Justin had spiked that drink with something.

Our next meeting was at Debbie's house. Justin started the meeting by asking each of us on a scale of one to ten, what our energy level was for working on ourselves. This was a question he asked us often, and each time I felt like an idiot having no idea what number to say. But today something had shifted in me, and I could feel that I had it, I had a lot of energy for working on myself. So, I said ten. Everyone else was five or lower.

Tom said, "I feel that you," and he pointed at me, "are kidding yourself."

Justin said, "So, what's the 'I feel that I?'"

Tom looked confused for a moment, then his face went into an agonized look. "Oh jeez, okay, right." He had a very expressive face; each emotion that passed through him found its way into the lines around his eyes and mouth.

As opposed to Dan, who had one of those faces that would have been great in a poker game, since it told you nothing about what he was feeling.

I said to Dan, "I feel that you never show what you are feeling."

Tom said, "Hey, wait a minute, I'm not done." He looked at me accusingly. "Okay, so, I ... feel ... that ... I ..."

He frowned and grimaced and expressed frustration and resignation and soul-searching. Then he shook his head violently. He was stuck, which is what seemed to happen with all of us when Justin asked what seemed to be a simple question.

"Well first, it's like this, I feel that John thinks he's better than all of us. So that means that I must feel that he is *not* better than us. I feel that I am better than him!"

Justin said, "Don't over-complicate it. What was the feeling?"

Tom shouted, "I feel competitive. How's that? Is that it?"

Justin nodded his head. "Good, that's good. Remember, it's all about you." He pointed at Tom.

"And it's all about you." He pointed at Debbie, "and you and you and you and you," he said, pointing at each one of us.

"It's all about what you are feeling, what you are thinking, what's happening inside of you. The work is about directing your attention inwards. Instead of blaming what's out here, you recognize what you are feeling. No one or thing out here can make you feel anything, unless *you* let it."

Then he said, "So, let's talk about the chanting. Some observations about it, what did you guys experience?"

I realized that I would have to say something about my sexual desire for Mona since that really was the strongest experience I'd had at the chanting. And, needless to say, that terrified me. I hardly heard what people were saying, I was so overcome with a nervous feeling. Finally there was an opening, and I blurted out, "I felt a lot of sexual desire for Mona."

I meant to say more, like to relate it to the chanting or something to take the edge off, but nothing more came out.

Tom, Rick, and Rob laughed, or started to laugh before they caught themselves. Justin was stoic-faced in these meetings, and this moment was no different. He never let on what he was feeling.

In Ouspensky's book, G had said that negative emotions should not be expressed, so, I assumed that this is why Justin did not show much emotion in our meetings, that he was following that dictum.

I understood that advice as meaning that we have a limited amount of energy, and expressing negative emotions is a waste of energy, since usually expressing a negative feeling does absolutely no good in the real world. Yelling at a traffic jam never helps the traffic move along.

Although there was no response to my statement, and we were quickly onto something else, I did feel much better having said it out loud. In fact, I was surprised by how simple and easy it had been to say something that had made me so nervous.

Justin at the conclusion of the meeting said that we would be chanting at the Student Union the next Tuesday evening, which meant we would be inviting the public to join us. He told us to try and get there a little early so we could set up the room differently, make it more inviting for the chanting experience.

The next Tuesday, just as we were about to start chanting, Justin told me to go downstairs to a certain room where a spiritual group was scheduled to be watching a short movie. He told me to watch the movie and then make an announcement inviting people to come to the chanting. I was disappointed because that would mean I would miss the start of the chanting, but I did what he told me to do.

When I arrived in the room, it was crowded and dark; the movie was just starting from a movie projector. It was about a boy guru from India named Guru Maharaj Ji. He was the one I'd heard about. the one Jane's daughter Melissa followed. The one that the guy with the short hair wearing a tie had told me about on the street, and whom I had read about in the newspaper in D.C. the year before.

I quickly became absorbed in the film. It was entertaining and well done, moved along quickly, starting with the story of the boy's father, who had been a guru. When he died, he transmitted his power to his youngest of four sons with the instructions to take *The Knowledge* to the world. *The Knowledge* was a meditation technique that put you in touch with the energy inside you. They referred to it as the primordial vibration, the *holy name* or *word* of God. The movie had a great soundtrack, rock bands playing original songs, devotional rock songs to the guru, and people in the room enthusiastically joined in during certain songs.

The boy guru was shown arriving in London and then in New York City, met by people who appeared to be in ecstasy, bowing down and putting flowers around his neck, and generally going absolutely berserk in his presence. It reminded me of the time I saw the Beatles. When they came out on stage the place erupted, girls screaming at the top of their lungs, girls fainting. I also felt an excitement, but, being a guy, certainly not enough to scream and tear my hair. That was something girls did, but not the guys.

However, for Guru Maharaj Ji it was not just the females, it was everyone, including old men. Those displays of devotion were quite unsettling to me. I thought of that couple who had picked me up hitchhiking, and their giggling about sending a package to their guru. The language in the film was weird, words and phrases like s*urrender, blissed out, devotion, perfect master, holy name of God, divine light, primordial vibration, premie.*

One phrase in particular impressed itself on my brain: *Truth is the Consciousness of Bliss*. I had never considered truth could be the awareness of bliss. I had to admit that idea appealed to me very much.

And another phrase made me uncomfortable: *a guileless heart.* "Guru Maharaj Ji will only reveal the Knowledge of God to the sincere seeker of truth who has a guileless heart."

I sure as hell knew that could not be me!

And, strangest of all, when the guru appeared in the film I felt his presence on a physical level. I felt a rush, a vibration, a shift in my awareness, much like I had felt when at thirteen, I first saw the Beatles on television.

When the movie ended - it was only about 20 minutes long - I had a big grin on my face and I was swept up in the goofy, happy vibes in the room.

However, I remembered why I was there and went to the front of the room and made my announcement about chanting. I felt silly making the announcement because it was obvious these people had found something better than chanting.

I then joined the others chanting. It was almost polar opposite for me to the previous night of chanting. I could not let go to the chanting. I felt stuck in my head, like I was looking at myself chanting and thinking how idiotic it was. And I was glad when we ended early.

The next weekend there was a party at Dan and Mona's commune in the country. My plan was to hitchhike there and my first ride was a woman in a VW who had a picture on the dashboard of her car. I became curious about that picture, something looked familiar about it.

"Who's that?" I asked.

Her face broke into a huge grin. "Groomaraji." Then she started giggling.

I didn't really understand what she was saying but I then knew this had to be the same guru I had seen in the movie. I was intrigued. "I saw that movie about him, do you have the Knowledge?"

"Yes, I do."

"What's it like?"

She started talking and her words flowed out effortlessly and passionately.

"It's a feeling of energy, energy inside. It's the most beautiful feeling of knowing something inside you, having a connection, a feeling that never stops or ends and it's inside you, and it is to you, and it is God. It puts you in touch with God inside you. God is not somewhere else out there somewhere. Energy cannot be created and cannot be destroyed, the energy is constantly there inside us to connect with. And the energy is a vibration, the word of God that the Bible speaks of. In the beginning was the word and the word was with God and the word was God. That word is inside of us, right now, all the time, keeping us alive. And there's a light, the light of God, and a sound …"

She talked non-stop, I swear, the entire way to Dan and Mona's party. Somehow she was able to drive with her hands waving around expressively as she talked. Her name was Carol, and how strange it was to realize that she was going to the same party I was. However, she didn't know anyone there; she had been invited by a friend to meet her there.

I felt giddy getting out of the car; her words had made me high, but I could also feel an opposite part of me forming a very negative opinion about all this silly guru talk. This part of me was very suspicious, thinking she was just another religious fanatic. Same as a Jesus freak, just a more modern version - a teenage guru freak.

And that was not what I wanted!

At the party there were kegs of beer, grass, food, people playing guitars, beautiful long-haired women and men. Everything one would expect to see at a party on a commune in the springtime, except to me it also felt in some way like a frat house party. People looked and dressed differently, but it was the same vibe. Feel good by consuming to excess.

Justin and his wife Merle were also there. Perhaps their presence made me realize how little interest I had in the general activities of the party. I introduced Carol to them.

Carol had a blissed-out smile permanently attached to her face. She said hello and then she took out a button of her guru and put it on her shirt. It was a psychedelic one with flashing colors depending on which angle you saw it. Merle asked her about the button. Carol was very happy to explain, she went into a long spiel about Guru Maharaja Ji and how his mission was to spread the Knowledge to the world and that the way she could help was by exposing as many people as possible to his picture.

I was aware again of the split in me. One part of me was feeling very good, standing there listening to Carol even though the facts of what she said sounded weird, ridiculous, and way too simple. And another part could not believe she was actually wearing a button of her guru! How ridiculous! In other words, an I feel that you!

Justin asked her, "So, how does one go about receiving the Knowledge?

She said, "You become prepared to receive Knowledge by listening to satsang. I live in Portland, but there is a premie house in Eugene where there's satsang three times a week. That's the first step, hear more satsang. Satsang is what prepares you for Knowledge. Sat means truth and sang means company of. Satsang is the company of truth and it will make you more thirsty for the Knowledge…"

Justin interrupted her before she would speak for another 15 minutes. "And who gives the Knowledge?"

She said, "Groomraji does not reveal the Knowledge himself. He has mahatmas touring America who reveal the Knowledge. Maha means great and atma is soul. They are great souls and they are on the earth now to help Groomraji with his mission. One will probably be coming to Eugene this summer. So, start going to satsang and by summer you will probably be able to receive it."

I didn't think much of all this. I didn't really see myself going to satsang, whatever that was. It seemed like something interesting to hear about, but I was not about to attend some kind of religious service three times a week.

At our next group meeting, Justin announced that we would be going to a house across town to hear satsang. Of course I knew what he was talking about, but the others didn't know and someone asked what it was. Justin was his typical stoic self and said we would find out when we got there. He also instructed us to walk in silence. It was about a twenty-minute walk, and when we got there it was a typical middle class home in a middle class neighborhood. We were instructed to take our shoes off and leave them by the door. The house was unusually clean, spotless really, and we filed in and sat on the floor facing an altar with many, many pictures of the guru on it.

The meeting seemed to be exclusively for us, as we were the only new people there. Three women, who I assumed lived in the house, all spoke, or gave satsang. I was particularly struck by one woman's talk, Michele. Michele appeared to be in a genuine state of rapture as the words flowed out of her. She spoke about her life before she learned how to meditate and about how different it was now that she was meditating. Just walking down the street she fell in love with people because she saw that the same energy inside of her was inside of them. And looking at her, I could see that she radiated a feeling of love. There was no denying she was feeling something I had never been in touch with before.

They put on a record and played a very silly song, which they sang along to. Something about getting to heaven, and getting your sins taken away. Any kind of religious song that mentions sins and heaven was sure to turn me off, but for some reason this song did not. I was mystified by my reaction. I tried to ignore it, but the reality was I felt something really nice in the presence of these premies - which by the way, was another annoying word. A premie is a lover of God, and the followers of this guru called themselves premies.

Soon I was singing along. I got a taste of the nice feeling of mindlessly singing a silly song with a bunch of other people - except most of the people in the room were not singing along. Looking around I saw that the others in my group were not being affected the way I was. I realized I was no longer attending the meeting as an observer. I was merging with it, and I felt slightly guilty about that, like I was going into this thing way too quickly. Even though Justin had not given us any instructions about what to do at this meeting, I felt odd getting so caught up in the vibe.

Justin had us walk home in silence also and during that walk I pondered the strange similarity between Michele with her beatific smile, and a Jesus Freak girl I had once met on the street who had tried to get me to ask Jesus to come into my heart. Most Jesus freaks were into talking about sin, or about how to be saved, or were into quoting the Bible verbatim, but this girl was all about the love of Jesus. Michele reminded me so much of that kind of Jesus Freak. Same kind of nice soft voice, same kind of beautiful, loving smile, same kind of authentic display of an inner feeling which I was certain was not being faked.

At the next group meeting, Justin asked us to rate from one to ten our interest in what we had heard last week about Guru Maharaj Ji and his Knowledge.

As we went around the room, most of the numbers were from one to four; Mona gave it a seven, and when it was my turn I said, ten. Tom scoffed incredulously.

"You have got to be kidding," he almost shouted.

I was about to react when Justin said, "Explain. Why a ten?"

I said, "Well, one big goal I have is to learn how to meditate. These people seem to be experiencing something from the meditation they are doing, what they call the Knowledge, and I want to check it out. They are not toting Bibles around, they have nothing but what they are experiencing inside, and they seem to be able to talk endlessly about it, so I want to know more, I want to find out if I can feel the vibration, see the light, all that. That's why I give it a ten."

Tom asked, "But how do you know they are really experiencing any of it, and not just repeating like parrots what they heard someone else say?"

As usual Tom annoyed the hell out of me, "I *don't* know, Tom, that's why I want to check it out. It sounds too good to be true, I know, but still, I can't just write it off as impossible. I mean, I am looking for the miraculous. And aren't we all, in search of the miraculous? So, if the miraculous appears, I can't then say, oh, that's impossible!"

Tom looked at me like he was trying very hard to be nice.

Mona said, "Justin, you didn't give it a number. What about you, what do you give it?" Justin said, "As an answer to that, I have an announcement. I'm going to Denver to check this thing out. You are all welcome to come with me. I plan to leave in 3 days."

He looked around. "Questions?"

I immediately said, "Yeah, I want to go. But why Denver?"

"Denver is the headquarters and that would be the best place to check it out. There are several people there who are giving the Knowledge to people."

The room was silent. Mona spoke up, "I want to go."

Dan said nothing. I wondered how that would work out, since they had a two-year-old to take care of.

No one else said anything. Justin said, "Okay, so, John and Mona so far. Give me a call if you change your mind or if you have any questions. You two, give me a call tomorrow, and I will give you more details."

Chapter 10

Walking home after that meeting, I was in shock. The direction my life was going in had suddenly become completely unpredictable. And I marveled at the synchronicity of Denver as our destination for finding truth. I had been a big Jack Kerouac fan and in his first great book, *On the Road*, Denver is hugely significant.

When I told Alonzo I would be leaving, he was very disappointed. I reminded him that I would be returning in probably a few weeks. He was skeptical; I think he figured that once I received the Knowledge of God he would never see me again. We'd just had our debut at the Odyssey Café, and he was hoping to set up more performances for us. For me the experience had been anti-climactic. I had been nervous but not overly so, and I had been able to play and even enjoy myself. I thought it was fun, but I was now completely focused on finding out more about the Guru Maharaj Ji experience, and didn't think twice about abandoning my music partner.

The day of departure came. Justin showed up in a van with another van behind him. There would be seven adults and three children in two vans. Justin and Merle and their little baby boy; Dan and Mona and their two-year-old son, Mr. B; and a friend of Justin's visiting from the east coast, Bob, along with his five-year-old daughter.

And, what a surprise, at the last minute Tom jumped into the van.

The trip took longer than usual partly because we had three young children along, but Justin made a point of using the trip as an opportunity to work on overcoming mechanical behavior. As his exercises had demonstrated, one approach to combat mechanical behavior is to simply do things a little differently than one normally does them.

On this trip from Eugene to Denver, about 1300 miles, the expected way to make the trip was to go as quickly as possible, to stop only when necessary. That's how Kerouac had traveled with his buddy Neal Cassidy. Their creed was to go as fast as possible, and don't stop till you get there. And after all, we were going to Denver to check out what might be the Knowledge of God. We'd better not delay!

Justin had us do almost the opposite; we stopped frequently, and there was plenty of grumbling about it. Certainly, whenever I had traveled I had usually gone as far as possible each day and rested only when absolutely necessary. I viewed traveling as a means to an end, not an end in itself.

To put the brakes on that momentum was a new experience for me, and I liked it. I found it seductive and liberating. I was no longer held hostage by the need to get to where I was going. I was given permission to be *here* even though *here* was not of any immediate apparent interest. Taking the time to stop in a random rest area was like cheating, stealing a segment of time that normally I would not have allowed myself to have.

To fully appreciate my feelings on this trip, I would need to tell you my life story leading up to this time, but I'm sure you can appreciate that I found it magical and amazing to be traveling with ten other people seeking a mysterious *Knowledge* from a teenage guru. And it probably helped that I was not *that* eager to get to Denver. I knew what lay in wait in Denver: more strange satsang from unusually happy people. I was more than content to be on the journey, to be a seeker, and I was not in any hurry to have it end. To be taking a step like this was a destination in and of itself. After all, I had come out west to find something dramatic and wonderful, and it was happening.

At one such stop along the way Justin, Dan and I got into a conversation about spiritual schools. In the first book we had read out loud together, *Mount Analogue*, one of the characters in the book told a story about being at a spiritual school. And in the book *In Search of the Miraculous*, the teacher G gives quite a long description of various types of spiritual schools. Dan asked Justin if he knew of any.

Justin said that he did.

Now this was more information than Justin would usually let out. Whenever a question came up about Justin's past, he usually revealed nothing, maintaining an air of mystery. However, we were not able to get more out of him about the school he knew about, but he did say that he could not return to that school until he brought some people along with him.

This led into a conversation about the three centers of human beings: the intellectual, emotional, and physical centers. We had read about these centers in reference to schools, the idea being that different schools focused on different centers. While I easily understood the idea of the three centers, I had no first-hand experience or knowledge of them.

Dan was wondering what center he usually operates from, which he thought was important because supposedly this was also a clue into one's *level of being*, another concept I had no real experience or understanding of, and also what kind of school he should be seeking. I gave Dan my opinion, which was that he was usually coming from his intellectual center. Dan had enough sense not to give me his opinion of me, but I was also quite sure that I was usually operating from the intellectual center. I figured since I was always thinking, I must be operating from my intellectual center.

Justin though was quick to tell me that I definitely operated from the emotional center. I was skeptical. He said, "Well, you may not be expressing those emotions and you may think you're not an emotional person, but if you think about what makes you do the things you do, it is your feeling center."

Of course this was exactly right, but I was blind to my own behavior and motivations. Later, I would realize the obvious fact that the guru experience was something I responded to on a *feeling* level. I liked it because it made me *feel* good. The ideas put forward were simplistic, designed for an uneducated person to understand, but I was able to overlook that because I liked the *feeling* it gave me.

After a few days of traveling we arrived in Salt Lake City after dark. On a bulletin board we found the address of a halfway house in town that would put up travelers, and discovered upon entering the house that it was a Christian house, similar to a house of Jesus freaks in Eugene.

Once we entered the house we were set upon by many Bible-carrying people milling about. It was like an alternate reality. Not only were there many people hanging around in the living room, each carrying at least one bible, but there was the largest bible I have ever seen on a table. I did not want to appear curious about it, but I really wanted to see if I could even lift it. Then one girl zeroed in on me. She was pretty, her name was Mary, and I was more than willing to have her talk to me. She was exactly the kind of Jesus Freak that reminded me of Michele, the premie in Eugene. She was all about feeling the love, and Mary was definitely feeling the love of Jesus. I must have looked especially receptive. She took my hand and led me into a quiet bedroom and we sat on the lower half of a bunk bed, and she asked me to open my heart to Jesus.

I was for sure feeling the love. Mary was beautiful, like a saint really, as she held both my hands in hers and looked deeply into my eyes. Then she closed her eyes and prayed to Jesus.

"Oh Jesus, oh Savior divine, please come into John's heart, please oh Lord, open John's heart to you, oh Jesus, open his heart to you.

"John," she opened her eyes, "would you let Jesus into your heart, would you like to feel the love of Jesus in your heart, right now?"

How could I say no?

I couldn't, so I said nothing.

Mary went to her trusted Bible for her next round of ammunition. She opened the book looking for a passage.

Before she could get going with that, I decided I needed to represent myself in some kind of truthful way. I tried an argument I had tried on Jesus freaks in Eugene, never with much success, but I still liked my argument too much to stop using it.

"Wait, Mary, what about this? Jesus did not have a Bible with him when he was teaching. None of that had been written yet. He spoke from his own experience, not from quoting a Bible. And he was not telling his followers, his disciples to read the Bible. He never says in the Bible that we should be reading the Bible. I know Paul says it, but Paul never even met Jesus. So, since Jesus was not teaching his disciples to read the Bible, what was he teaching them to do?"

I thought that was a pretty damn good question, but being a good Jesus Freak she had a pretty damn good answer and responded, "Jesus knew he could not be here physically with all of us so he gave us the Bible to use to contact him. He is with us through the Bible - the word of God is for us, the Bible."

I said, "But I don't want a substitute, I want the real thing, I want to meet a living Master."

That got her attention, real fast.

"Jesus is Lord, Jesus is Lord, Jesus is Lord," she said warily. I'd heard Jesus freaks in Eugene say this when their faith was challenged. It was a surefire way to ward off the devil.

"Oh, John, don't become a victim of a false prophet. They will lead you directly to hell, John. What in the world do you mean, a *living* master?"

"I mean, someone alive now. Jesus at one time was alive now, right? Wouldn't you prefer to meet Jesus alive instead of just, in the Bible?"

"Jesus is Lord, Jesus is Lord, Jesus is Lord. Is that why you are going to Denver? To meet a living Master?" She said it with such disdain, I knew then and there this was a hopeless situation.

"Who is this so called living master?"

"His name is Guru Maharaj Ji. He is a …"

But she didn't let me finish; frantically, she started praying.

"Jesus is Lord, Jesus is Lord. Oh Jesus, please Jesus, help John, give John your guidance."

Then she gave up on praying to Jesus and decided to confront me directly. She opened her eyes, let go of my hands and stood up in front of me.

"John, you need to listen to me. That is a false prophet you are chasing after. It was predicted in the Bible. False prophets are the instruments of the devil. How can you believe in such a thing? It's predicted in the Bible, let me read it to you."

"Mary, listen to me. It's already been read to me. I don't care what the Bible says. because I don't believe in the Bible."

As I was speaking she was moving farther and farther away from me. I could tell she now saw me as a representative of the devil, but throwing caution to the wind, I tried my last round of ammunition. "I want to ask you something. How can you believe that the word of God is an actual word on a page? The word of God is in your heart."

"That's exactly right, John. And the word of God is Jesus, not some guru. 'And the word was made flesh and dwelt among us.' That's from John, 1:14. Jesus is the word and he is in your heart right now. You don't have to go to Denver to feel the word of God."

Then she knelt down on the floor, closed her eyes, and wailed. "Oh Jesus, I know John is sincere, but he is being tempted by false prophets. He needs your mercy now, oh Jesus, please enter his heart, please, John, will you pray with me now. You don't need to go to Denver to find God, God is right here in Salt Lake City."

She held out her hand to me to join her on the floor, to try one more time to pray to Jesus, but I could not continue the charade.

She left the room and I soon went to bed.

The next morning when I climbed into the van, Justin said, "Well, I thought maybe I was gonna lose our first born when I saw you disappear into the bedroom with that girl."

I said nothing.

Justin said, "Did you have to tell her that we are going to Denver to see a guru? You are aware that you can always lie, right?"

I looked at him stupidly.

Merle added, "Really, John, I had three different people come up to me and try to convince me not to go. They surrounded me, all holding their bibles. It was like some kind of horror movie, these zombines coming after me with their bibles! I can't believe you would tell them that we are going to see a Guru from India, my god, in a house full of those people!"

I mumbled, "Uh, yeah, sorry, really, that was… uh…"

Mona was giggling, "What were you doing, trying to get that pretty girl to come along with you to Denver?"

I looked at her with daggers in my eyes. And with the full realization that I may have actually had that idea.

Mona said, "I just tell them I'm already saved. But then you kinda blew it for me once they found out where we were all going. Thanks a lot." And she gave me a playful shove.

I said, "Okay, I am sorry, I really am, that was dumb."

Justin said, "Stop apologizing. The thing is to learn something."

I tried to think what I could learn from this.

He went on, "And I don't mean, learn to not do it again. Not that kind of learning."

Silence as we made our way through the streets of Salt Lake City to the freeway.

"So, I'm not getting what I can learn from this. Other than don't tell a house full of Jesus that we are going to see a guru from India."

He said, "Well, think about yourself, and how you behaved with that girl. What does that tell you about you?"

Mona started giggling again.

Justin said, "Mona, shut up."

So then I started laughing because I looked at Mona and she had her cheeks all puffed out like she was trying so hard to not say something.

Finally I said, "Okay, I am susceptible to pretty girls inviting me into their bedrooms. For any reason, even to pray to Jesus."

Justin nodded his head, "Okay, that's a start. Go on. What else?"

He prompted me, "What I am talking about is that you told her you were going to Denver."

"Right, well, I don't even think of lying. I tell the truth. I think it's important to tell the truth."

"Okay, so, tell me, what's that all about?"

"What do you mean?"

"I mean, tell me why you think it's so important to tell the truth. Do you think it's truth with capitol T?"

I was incredulous. "Seriously? I mean, aren't we all supposed to tell the truth?"

"Supposed to? Says who?"

I took a deep breath. "Okay, so I was raised to believe that telling a lie is a sin. So, I guess that's where it came from, my wanting to tell the truth."

Justin said, "Okay. But look, let's get away from the morality issue, right or wrong, all of that. I'm not talking about that. I'm not trying to teach you to tell lies, as if that is some wonderful thing to do. I am trying to get you to see something else, another perspective. You are a collection of selves. Right? There is no such thing as John, as one united self. I mean, there is no such self as John, as one self. John, the collection of selves, has a self interested in seeking truth, in learning how to meditate. But John also has a self interested in playing music, in sleeping, in going into a bedroom with a girl to pray to Jesus, in doing all kinds of things that have nothing to do with meditating or seeking truth. Are you with me so far?"

"Yeah." I was feeling very nervous about where this was going.

"So, I maintain that the very idea of truth is a useless and pointless construct. It's all relative to which self is speaking. What is the truth for one self is the opposite of the truth for another self."

He was silent for a moment.

I said, "Okay, yeah, I understand that, although it seems to me that the self that was speaking was the self that was interested in going to Denver and seeking truth, so that's why it spoke."

"Yeah, so what? I mean, that's right, but what I am trying to impress upon you is to have an awareness of how fleeting a self that is, in the moment, ya know? So then it would be easier, given the situation that we were in a house full of Jesus freaks, to realize the absurdity of telling them where we were going. If you understand how there is no truth with a capital T, then maybe it would be easier for you to speak from another self. In other words, give a different version of *the truth*. You are traveling for the fun of it. Because you do have a self that is doing this just for the sheer fun and excitement of it. Am I right?"

"Wow. Yeah, that is true. I get that."

He went on, "In a way, there is no truth and there also is no lie. Because whatever you say, there is a self in you for whom what you say is true."

Mona raised her hand.

Justin, who was driving, saw her in the rear view mirror.

"Yes, Mona, you can now speak. I did not intend for you to be quiet the rest of the trip, although that might be an interesting experiment for you."

"Don't even think of that! No, I want to say thank you for saying all that. I appreciate it. It really makes sense. 'Cause I was also raised a Catholic. And it is interesting to think of lying and telling truth as relative to what self is speaking. I mean, right now? I am so happy Mr. B is in the other van with Dan, cause that means I get to listen to this conversation, you know? So, this self up in me now is not a mother, it has no interest in being a mother. So, I can say, and it is not a lie, that I like not being a mother."

I could not help but notice a big change in how I was behaving. As I have mentioned I did not live with any of these people I was traveling with and had only known them for a relatively short time. On this trip we could not help but become closer. For one thing, I could no longer pretend to be "together" or "spiritual " or "clever". All that stopped because it was impossible to keep that up hour after hour, all day long. We all just became simply who we were. A certain number of hours and days in a car will do that to a person. If you want to get to know someone, take a long car trip with them.

One of the ways we entertained ourselves was by singing. Dan was a good guitar player, and we sang Beatles songs and popular hits of the time. One of our favorites was John Denver's "Colorado Rocky Mountain High," which was getting a lot of radio play at that time, and it seemed to have been written specifically for us on our journey.

At some point just south of Cheyenne, as Justin pulled off the road yet again for an unnecessary stop, Tom left the van and stuck out his thumb. He was tired of our endless delays and eager to get on to Denver. I felt almost the opposite. I was thoroughly enjoying being with everyone, goofing off with the kids, talking with Justin, singing.

When we finally did pull into the parking lot of the ashram in Boulder, we had been traveling for a number of days. And there right in front of us, about to get into a car, was a bald-headed, orange-robed holy man from India, a mahatma.

He pointed at us and said something to someone. Then he was shouting something at us. We hurried out of the vans, eager to hear this directive from the man we had come to see. Had he been expecting us? Did he know who we were? My mind was spinning, imagining the possibilities, what important message he would have for us.

What a shock it was to hear that he was shouting, "Go home! Go home!" Then he got into the car and it drove away.

Mindlessly, we turned to get back into the van. After all, we had come here to see the orange-robed mahatma, and he told us what to do next, he was giving us direct orders. How could we ignore him?

But then a guy who had been with the mahatma before he got into the car, hurried over and said, "Hey wait, don't leave yet, first come to the program."

We asked why the mahatma had told us to go home, and he answered, "Mahatma-ji saw your license plates are from Oregon. Guru Maharaj Ji does not want people traveling to receive the Knowledge. He wants them to stay where they are and get ready where they are living. But since you have come all this way, you should at least come to the program."

So we went to the program. The program consisted of premies singing songs and speaking, giving satsang. A few premies spoke first. They looked to be about my age and were well dressed and groomed. I was very impressed by their being able to speak in front of a large number of people. And I was affected by their obvious sincerity and the depth of the feeling they were speaking about and also seemed to be experiencing first hand. And the fact that they spoke with no notes made it all the more impactful. They would close their eyes, meditate for a moment, and then open their eyes and out the words would flow.

Then the big guns, the bald mahatmas in orange robes spoke. I did not relate much to the mahatmas' talks, though it was interesting just looking at a priest from India, considered the world's great holy land. One problem was the language and cultural barrier, and more importantly, the mahatmas tended not to tell personal stories. I preferred the heartfelt words from the premies. It could be edge-of-the-seat exciting listening to a premie speak from the heart. And, it could also be mind-numbingly dull when the premie simply repeated phrases or when the mahatmas told spiritual stories from the Indian culture over and over again.

At the conclusion of the program someone announced that those interested in receiving Knowledge should go to the ashram. A mahatma would be there to choose who would be in the next day's Knowledge session.

We didn't even think of driving back to Eugene as the mahatma had ordered us to do; we were going to the ashram to see if we could get the Knowledge.

On the ride there Mona talked about the incredible auras she had seen around the mahatma.

"It was bright pink, and then in his talk it became green."

"All around him?"

"All around him, well, maybe not his feet but most of his body was generating a pulsing color field."

"I sure didn't see anything."

"Well, did you try?"

"No."

"Try to look at what is happening around his body and his head. I bet you will see something."

And as a matter of fact, I did see colors around the speakers from then on. It was mildly interesting to focus on the colors when the words were boring, but I did not understand the point of it, other than to amuse myself when I was tired of listening to the words.

When we got to the ashram, the room was packed with people sitting on the floor. I sat in the back thinking it was the only place available, although I did notice that some people who came in late just plowed their way to the front and made themselves room. A premie was giving satsang, basically repeating all the stories that the mahatma had told. I'd had enough satsang for one night. Physical discomfort and mental boredom started to set in. Then the mahatma arrived, and people started shouting at him, begging him to choose me, choose me, pick me mahatma-ji!

I was amazed and more than a little disappointed. I couldn't believe this is what it was all about. It seemed so uncivilized, rude, disorganized as well as so unspiritual, or maybe I mean un-meditative. It was pandemonium. I knew it would be impossible for me to shout out and demand the mahatma to choose me to receive the Knowledge.

The mahatma did not seem to know much English either. So his questions to people were pretty simple.

"Do you have an open heart?"

How can someone answer that? People did though, basically just saying how much they wanted

Knowledge and much they wanted to serve, and how much they loved Guru Maharaja Ji.

Another question, "Why do you want the Knowledge?"

I thought, this is absurd. Why *wouldn't* someone want the Knowledge? Why wouldn't someone want the connection inside to God's pure and perfect energy?

And the Mahatma did not seem to pay much attention when they answered. He'd simply smile and then call on someone else, or he would give more satsang.

Needless to say I was not picked to receive Knowledge. I never even raised my hand.

We found a place to crash that night, and the next day we went to a house that was having satsang. We sat in a huge living room knee to knee for a long time. I was waiting, along with everyone else. We were all waiting for someone to come and give satsang to us, we were mostly newbies, wannabes. So, I was in this mode of waiting, sitting passively and waiting for something to happen to me, or for me.

A former student of Justin's, Rob, who I had met at the Tuesday night meetings in Eugene, had just moved to Boulder to study under a Zen Buddhist teacher. The only thing I knew about this teacher in Boulder was that he had his students drink a lot of beer.

Justin had told Rob we were in town to check out Guru Maharaj Ji, and so Rob showed up on this morning at this house. He came in and sat in the living room for a little while and then said to everyone, "How is everyone doing? I feel a little strange."

No one responded, everyone looked embarrassed. I knew Rob was speaking up because it was probably very confronting for him to speak up in a living room full of strangers. He was working on himself, and I felt bad that I could not help support his efforts, but I also recognized that I didn't have the same aim. I was in this passive mode of waiting to find out what this Guru Maharaj Ji trip was all about.

Finally, a guy got up and started to give satsang. He sat in a chair and very intensely spoke to us about the word of God.

"The Word of God is within you, it is not in the scriptures, the scriptures say there is a word of God. Now, we think the scripture is the word of God. It's not the Word of God. The Word of God came long before there was language. The word of God is a vibration that goes on inside us, has always been there and will always be there, regardless of whether we are aware of it or not. This is the Name of God, the holy name of God is not Ram, is not Krishna, is not Mohammed, is not Jesus, is not Buddha. People think that by chanting the name of Krishna that one can be saved, because Krishna said, whoever remembers my name, that person will be with me. But the name is not Krishna, it is within you now, how could it not be?"

He went on for quite a while. I followed his line of reasoning and was impressed that none of this had occurred to me before, and it made sense to me, and I'd already heard variations on this same theme at previous satsangs.

But then the next guy went on in the same vein for quite a while and I became bored. It was interesting for maybe thirty minutes, but then, not that interesting. I wanted to experience it, not hear about it. And also I was vaguely aware that there was something unattractive about everyone's behavior having been modified in the way it had been modified. It was like I was looking in on a set of a play going on. Everyone was playing a role in accordance with everyone else's roles, which were all in line with the rules of this particular organization.

And I knew it was not attractive to me. I didn't want to become like these premies.

Justin found us an entire apartment we could stay in and we entered into the routine of going to the ashram during the day and seeing if we could help with any household chores, and then at night attending the satsang programs, which were in various locations around Denver and Boulder. Then after all that, we went to the late night sessions at the ashram when the mahatma would pick the next group to receive Knowledge.

There was a lot going on inside me. For one thing the initial excitement I'd felt from doing something so new and different wore off. Reality set in. At certain times in the programs I would feel that beautiful feeling which I had first felt watching the movie about the Guru, a feeling of being on the verge of something stupendous. This would certainly inspire me to keep trying. However, along with this occasional transcendent feeling, I also was going crazy with boredom. I was extremely critical of certain things that were happening, and I was also aware of my self being critical. I was aware to a certain extent of these different reactions in me to what was going on, but not feeling strongly enough in the negative way to leave. I was curious what it was really all about. Were they under a mass hypnosis? They really did look, sometimes, like they were having a real experience, a very attractive experience, an experience of bliss. And other times, some of them looked like they were as bored as I was.

I also did try to remember and practice what I had been learning in Justin's group. But it was hard to reconcile the two paths. The Guru Maharaja Ji path was complete in and of itself, it *claimed* that you could practice any religion and still receive Knowledge, but realistically, how could anyone have time? There seemed to be no separation between the meditation practice and a full on commitment to the organization. And that was the basic dilemma for me. I knew I did not want to join the organization; that was not appealing. Yet the more I listened to satsang, the more I was getting the message that you could not really practice Knowledge and achieve the state of bliss it promised unless one was fully immersed in helping Guru Maharaja Ji with his mission to spread Knowledge to the world.

I gradually over the course of the next week realized I needed to either quit trying to receive Knowledge or radically change my attitude, my strategy, if I actually had a strategy.

My self-talk went something like this:

"Okay, look, you really do want to meditate, so what's the big deal about asking for Knowledge?"

"Well, maybe it shouldn't be a big deal but it is. It's tough, I just don't have the guts to do what these people are doing. I need to do something to get noticed. I have to get myself to the front of the room, I need to be aggressive and push my way through. I need to raise my hand, and shout out while raising my hand. And I can't do that. I am not that kind of person."

"But wait, you first better have something to say. Something that sounds good."

"Oh, come on, that's bullshit! What does it matter whether I say something clever or not? The mahatma can't understand English enough to know anyway."

"Agreed, maybe the mahatma won't be able to understand, but everyone else in the room will know if it's bullshit."

"Who cares about the people in the room?"

"You do!"

"Look, the real problem is that it has to be from the heart."

That realization stopped the self-talk in its tracks. But then a self figured out something to say.

"Look, don't make it complicated. It's simple, just tell him the truth, that you want Knowledge."

"No, I have to cry about it, I have to beg for it, and I'm not gonna do that!"

"Why not?"

"Because I have no feelings remotely like the kind that would inspire me to cry. Other than from boredom. I just don't care that much."

"Yeah, right. Why don't you just admit the real problem here. You are terrified of speaking in front of a room full of strangers. You are totally intimidated by the scene. That's the only reason you are having a problem with this whole thing."

My self-talk is filled with details that are partly true and partly false. Yes, I did have the problem of being afraid to speak in front of strangers, but on the other hand, I did not have a problem with speaking at Justin's meetings.

I had a much more serious problem: I did not understand what devotion had to do with meditation, and I was incapable of taking whatever nice feelings I had for the guru and morphing them into devotion. I mean, the devotion that some premies manifested was intense. I just could not go there.

My hang-up at that time was, because the Knowledge consists of meditation techniques, why do I have to express all this yucky devotional stuff, which I was not feeling, just so I can learn how to meditate?

No one was around to answer my questions, and really I didn't even know how to express the confusion I was feeling. The scene was filled with contradictions and the response to any question was to listen to more satsang and open your heart to Guru Maharaja Ji.

So in a way, it was like I was put right back into that halfway house in Salt Lake City with the Jesus freaks. Just open your heart, that's all you gotta do. Except instead of opening my heart to Jesus, I now needed to open it to a fifteen-year old Guru I had never seen.

The Knowledge was spoken of as the secret hidden knowledge that Jesus had revealed to his apostles, that every great Master had revealed to his devotees. In other words, this was extremely important and not to be taken lightly. In Satsang, certain stories were told repeatedly. Most of these stories had the message that to be ready to receive Knowledge one should want it more than one wants anything else in the world. To first search the four corners of the world for happiness. If, after doing that, one is still dissatisfied, then come to him for the Knowledge. The idea being that only then would you understand its true value.

This revealed a contradiction because the Knowledge was being given out to people who had not even searched the four corners of the cities or towns they lived in. Those of us assembled to receive Knowledge were mostly about my age - in other words, young - and most of us had not done anything extraordinary to ready ourselves. Clearly, Guru Maharaj Ji was giving the Knowledge out to anyone who would show up and ask for it persistently enough.

Meanwhile, I could feel something building inside me. It was related to Justin's comment about the emotional center and that, regardless of whether I was aware of it, I was operating from it. That scared me because it seemed I was heading into unknown territory, and I seemed to be heading over the edge of a cliff. And I was either going to have to stop everything and go back to the life of my college town friends or continue on and go over the cliff. I knew I had no interest in going back to the college town and doing what all my college town friends were doing. So, that left going over the cliff as my only option.

But I did not know what going over the cliff meant, other than to somehow get changed into a highly emotional devotee. And as attractive as it looked in others, or as not attractive, it still felt like a million miles away from something I could ever feel. It reminded me of almost having a nervous breakdown in public.

I once attended a Chuck Berry concert and everyone in the auditorium was up out of their seat and dancing, except for me. For some weird reason I wasn't. It's not that I had never danced before. I had no problem dancing; usually, I liked to dance. But that night I just couldn't get my ass out of the chair. I was unwilling to join in the group mentality. Everyone else was dancing, maybe I felt like being different, maybe I was being obstinate and thinking I'm not gonna do what everyone else is doing. It was maybe a little bit of both, but the end result was I had a lousy time. Sure, I could tell myself that I sat there and enjoyed the music, and I did enjoy the music, but I could have *really* had a blast, going crazy dancing to a fantastic performer putting on a great show. But I didn't go *all the way.*

The evenings with the premies were reminding me more and more of that Chuck Berry concert. I was sitting there getting a certain something out of listening to the satsang and the music. But I was not going *all the way* into the experience. I was separate from what was happening, and a part of me understood that to get the Knowledge I needed to be one with it. I needed to get over this hump.

But practically speaking, what was I supposed to do? I didn't know if what I needed to do was bow down to the picture of the guru, or sing louder, or try to feel the desire in me, or break down and cry, what? A part of me wanted to let go, but how to let go?

And it seemed obvious to one part of me that I was simply not ready, but another part of me wanted to be ready. What did I need to do to break through into that feeling that other people were having? Even though the guru was not present, people were getting swept up, they were in an emotional frenzy, and I was just watching them.

I found myself wanting to distance myself from the people I had come with. A part of me blamed them: it was their fault. *They* were holding me back, it was *their* attitude of checking it out that was inhibiting me from going all the way. Checking it out implies keeping a certain distance from it, evaluating it. I didn't want to evaluate it. I wanted it. I wanted the Knowledge. So I started to sit by myself at the programs.

Then one night, Justin went over the cliff; he got swept away into a state of bliss that reminded me of the Hasidic saints I had read about in that book *Legends of the Baal Shem.* We were at one of the nightly programs, and I was doing my best to feel a part of the scene when I heard something going on in the aisle near me. I saw someone was on the floor in the aisle and seemed to be out of control, weeping loudly. Then I saw it was Justin. He was unable to stand, and a few people were trying to make sure he didn't hurt himself. I didn't know what had precipitated his going into another state of consciousness, I just saw him in the end state of being like a baby, crying loudly, unable to walk, helpless, a basket case.

I was dumbstruck. Justin had struck me as the ultimate observer, interested in simply checking out the experience but not interested in *having* the experience, and yet, there he was, he'd gone lock, stock and barrel into it. How in the world did he accomplish that? I had never seen Justin express much emotion anyway. He was always under control, not so much in an uptight way, but as the ultimate impartial observer of the human drama.

The only other one of our group who was passionately interested in receiving Knowledge was Mona. And she became the first of us to receive the Knowledge. She was picked one night to receive it in Denver. She seemed to have no qualms about pouring her heart out in front of a room full of strangers. I looked at her behavior and others who were begging and realized this was more of a leap than I had in me. It felt like the train was leaving the station without me, and I had no way of getting on it.

Chapter 11

Finally, the mahatma who was giving the Knowledge left Denver and started traveling west. He would be stopping at a series of communities and eventually would go through Eugene, some time in the next month. We learned his schedule and decided to try and meet up with him again in Salt Lake City. If that did not work out then we would go back to Eugene and be there when he came through. Bob and his daughter would not be coming with us, nor would Tom who decided to stay in Boulder, hoping to prepare himself to receive the Knowledge by doing service at the ashram. I was very surprised by the change that had taken place in Tom; he had started out so skeptical but had seemingly become a believer.

So, the rest of us, Dan, Mona, and their child, Justin, Merle, and their baby, and me got into the van and drove away.

As we drove out of town, I felt exhausted. I closed my eyes and tried to relax the only way I knew how which was to try not to think, to maintain a blank mind. Usually a futile exercise, and I really didn't even have the energy to try, but this time something changed. I began to complain to the powers of the universe about pretty much everything. It was fun to do, vent about all that was not right with the world, including the crazy organization of Guru Maharaja Ji. Then that gradually changed into begging for help from the universe at large, which soon morphed into begging for help from the guru.

The phrase "desperate times call for desperate measures" came to mind. I figured, why not try prayer? What have I got to lose? I'm like that rolling stone that Bob Dylan ranted about, out here in the world on my own, with no direction home, a complete unknown. I've got nothing, therefore I've got nothing to lose. Therefore, I may as well try anything, even praying to a fifteen-year-old guru whom I've never met.

And what can I say? I cannot lie about it. As much as it upset my apple cart to realize, the praying did produce a result. Something extraordinary happened. My thinking did not stop entirely - it was still there as faint background noise - but an emotion, a feeling, started to grow. I felt myself swirling inside into a most lovely inner state, my thoughts receding and becoming fainter as the feeling grew until it overwhelmed me completely.

I was sprawled in the back of the van with my eyes closed, and no one was paying any attention to me. I was able to lie there and just bask in a very beautiful feeling that in a way could be described as simply not having thoughts. Not thinking is nice in and of itself. At some point we stopped for gas and everyone was getting out, but I could not open my eyes and leave the experience I was having. This reminded me of how I had felt at the end of the movie *Panther Panchali*. Wow, I thought, it's happening again, that feeling is back!

When I finally did stumble out of the van, I was giggling, unable to contain the feeling of joy that was bubbling up. I didn't need to fake it, I didn't need to pretend; I was feeling it. I was finally *getting* that song, Amazing Grace! I now knew what Alonzo had been talking about.

It was all too strange to me, and it was all too new and I was too inarticulate in these matters to make some kind of general announcement to my traveling companions about what was happening with me. But something in me had cracked. When we got to Salt Lake City and Mahatma Parlokanand took his seat in the ashram living room, I was there directly in front of him with a big grin on my face. And it probably helped that there were not many people in the room. Salt Lake City had a tiny community compared to Denver. Mahatma started singing a devotional song, and I without hesitation joined in, feeling the meaning of the words all through my body. He smiled at me; he knew I was ready. When I asked to receive Knowledge he didn't ask me any questions, he patted my head affectionately and said in his broken English, "Most certainly, you may receive Knowledge."

And so Mary in the Jesus Freak house had been right all along. I would find God in Salt Lake City. But she was also wrong, because I'd had to leave. I had not been ready then.

The next day was the session in which I was initiated. When I was shown the four techniques, I experienced nothing, other than the strangeness of sitting in a darkened room with a small group of people and focusing my attention on the words of a bald-headed orange-robed man. I was disappointed at how simple the techniques were.

Why hadn't I already thought of this, I wondered? Yet, I knew I had not thought of it, and I also knew that no matter how many years I would live I would never have thought of it.

And while I was disappointed in their simplicity and by the lack of an immediate experience, I understood it was a practice, and I was eager to begin practicing. So much focus had been on pursuing this thing called Knowledge that I knew I would give it my best shot.

When we left Salt Lake City and headed back to Oregon, I realized my interest was not in getting back to Oregon. There was nowhere to go in the world that interested me but inside my self. I wanted to find out what it was I had been shown. Would meditating reveal to me the primordial vibration? Would I see the light of God, hear the divine music, taste the nectar of the gods? It was all so far-fetched, like I was living in an ancient fairy tale or a futuristic sci-fi movie. But I didn't want any more explanation about it, or theory, or words; I just wanted the experience, I wanted to know for myself.

We still stopped frequently, and at one rest area I went off by myself and meditated in the beautiful blossoming spring landscape of Idaho. It was there that it happened: what I had never been able to do before in meditation. I felt myself free from my thoughts. And replacing the connection to the thoughts was the connection to something simpler, my breath. The experience comes from something behind the breath, but for me, that first feeling of freedom from my thoughts was because I was able to connect *with* my breath, a flow happening inside me that I had did not have to create or maintain but which was always there.

It was truly nothing. No thoughts, no feelings, just an experience of awareness, awareness of something, which itself was really nothing. What is the sum amount of the awareness of your breath? It's nothing, right? But, it feels good, very good.

And, nothing is everything when thinking has gone away.

Another way to *not* describe it to say that my thoughts were replaced by a feeling of my *true self*. But the phrase *true self* is so pompous, and implies also the old religious duality of true and false, right and wrong, God and the devil. And using the word *feeling* is limiting, making it into something it is not. It is a feeling, and yet it is not a feeling like we normally think of feelings.

So, maybe feeling is the only way to describe it, but what is it a feeling of? It is a feeling of a feeling. And around and around we go!

Guru Maharaj-Ji used the word love to describe it. He would say in talking about the Knowledge, "Feel that love inside." And yes, I started to feel love for everyone, but not love the way I had always thought of love. Love is one of those words that can mean so many different things.

And to describe it as the primordial vibration makes a certain sense and also adds to the confusion. Primordial implies something in the past, this feeling is in the here and now and it is the most modern thing around. The word vibration does fit, but more in the sense of a *vibe*.

A vibe inside.

Another way to say it is that I felt present, or that I felt a presence inside me. I was in the here and now. I started laughing and staggered back to the van. Merle looked at me and smiled. She knew what had happened.

Then the van stopped working. We were stuck on the side of the road. We ended up staying with a man who opened his house to all of us while the van was being fixed. That night in the strange house, we were all feeling pretty drained and lifeless. We were in a rural area in Idaho, and there was nowhere to go even if we had the means to go.

Justin put on the premie record he had bought. Some of the songs were from the movie soundtrack, and there was one long song, "Spread this Knowledge," which was the one that did it to me every time I heard it. That song made me so emotional, and listening to it in that strange house brought me back into that feeling of being a premie, the feeling of having been given a secret, and that the secret needed to be shared with the world.

There was a growing split inside me. One side of me had gone over the cliff into this new experience of becoming a devotee of a guru, getting turned on by meditation. And yet, I still had my old self that, of course, had not gone over any cliff. It still thought and felt the same way it had always thought and felt. So, this old part of me was well aware of how weird my new life would become if I were to actually become a premie.

Returning to Eugene was anticlimactic. Justin told us he would not be leading the group anymore, nor would he be holding the meetings on Tuesday nights at the Student Union.

When I got home, Alonzo was happy to see me and after I told him I had learned how to meditate, he wanted to know if the guru was the one.

"The one what?" I asked.

"The messiah, the one who has been prophesied to come."

I was stunned to think that this was the expectation, and yet I knew that the premie scene in Denver certainly had promoted that very idea. On the street one day I ran into a guy from Justin's first group, and I could tell he was looking at me to see if I had changed, if I was now different, more enlightened or something. I was embarrassed because in the moment he saw me, I had been walking down the street lost in my thoughts. I was certainly not able to give him satsang, the way Carol or another premie would have been able to do. All I could do was mumble something about how the trip had gone.

I felt that I had been given something that at that moment was very small, a tiny seed. And I'd had that experience meditating by the side of the road, but that wasn't much to hang on to in the reality of every day life.

The mahatma that had given us Knowledge would be coming to Eugene soon and so we set up a table at the Student Union to hand out flyers about it. Sitting behind the table with Justin I had a very uneasy feeling. I was now officially putting myself out there for everyone to see as a follower of this teenage guru. I could feel myself sinking lower in my seat, trying to become invisible.

"Ya know what?" I said. "I'm terrified that I'm gonna see someone I know."

I held up something to try and cover my face, trying to make a joke out of it.

Justin laughed and said, "Premie!" He pointed at me and said loudly, "He's a premie!" I laughed and stood up and took a bow.

Of course no one paid any attention. They were all in the middle of their school day, rushing to a class, going to meet someone, or to grab something to eat.

I went to the local satsang in Eugene, but after experiencing all the energy and excitement in Denver, the small living room in Eugene with four other people did not allow me the anonymity I desired. After I told the others that, yes, I had been given the Knowledge, they naturally wanted me to say something, to give satsang. But I couldn't. That was still way beyond me. Walking home that night, I realized it was time to leave Eugene. I was stunned to think I had only been there about nine months. Still I knew my time was up. Whatever it was I had come out west to find, I had most certainly found it, and I knew my next step was to see the guru in person and then decide whether I wanted to get more involved in his organization.

Chapter 12

Guru Maharaj Ji was scheduled to appear at a festival in July in England, and I made it my priority to attend that festival. The charter flight was leaving from New York City, and so my plan was to first hitchhike to Minneapolis and stay with my brother Ben and work to earn money for the trip to London.

When I arrived at Ben's apartment, he wasn't home, but he had told me where he'd leave the key for me, so I let myself in. The first thing I wanted to do was to put my poster of Guru Maharaj Ji on the refrigerator. I did hesitate and think about it because, of course, it was not my kitchen, and I was also amazed at the condition of the kitchen. It was an unbelievable mess. I had not known this growing up, but I found out Ben did not clean up after himself. Every inch of counter space in his kitchen was covered with dirty dishes.

I had the thought, "Well, look at this place, why would Ben care? He wouldn't even notice!," even though I knew he would be sure to notice a poster on the refrigerator.

And then I had the thought, "But this kitchen is too messy, it would be disrespectful to put Guru Maharaj Ji's poster in a room that looks like this."

I shook my head as if to rid it of such a stupid thought. Did I now think of the poster as a sacred object, and that the image of Guru Maharaj Ji should not gaze down upon a messy kitchen?

Yes, as a matter of fact, a part of me *did* think that. Even though I had rejected the Catholic church and its teachings when I was 15, remnants of those teachings were still hanging around in my psyche waiting for a chance to emerge and impose their *should's* and *should-not's* into my behavior.

The poster was a picture of stars and planets filling a night sky with Guru Maharaj Ji's face superimposed onto it. The words said, "The energy that moves the universe moves you. Come and realize." I liked the decidedly cosmic and non-religious message, and since I had carried this poster all the way from Eugene, I wanted to put it up somewhere. I found some tape in one of the drawers and put the poster on the refrigerator door.

I had not been able to meditate on the trip so I was eager to sit. I looked around and decided the closet in the living room would be a good, dark place to meditate. I got myself settled in there and after a while, I heard someone open the front door and walk into the room, calling out to see if anyone was home.

"Hello," I called back, and opened the closet door and leaned out. It was a pretty girl with long dark hair.

"Hi. I'm Marie." She held out a piece of paper to me. I got myself up and out of the closet and looked at the paper. All it had on it was my brother's address.

"This is the right address. My name is John. Who are you looking for?"

She didn't answer; she seemed embarrassed, and I thought maybe it was because she was wondering what I had been doing in the closet.

I said, "I was meditating in there."

"Oh, really? Wow."

"This is my brother's apartment, his name is Ben. Is that who you are coming to see?"

"No, no, not him, a woman. I'm sorry, maybe I should come back some other time."

"Well, that's okay, would you like something to drink?"

I led her into the kitchen and quickly said, "I just got here a little while ago." I wanted to make sure she understood this messy kitchen was not my responsibility, and I was about to launch into some kind of lame excuse for the state of the kitchen, when she said, "Who is that?"

She was standing in front of the refrigerator pointing at the poster.

I laughed. It was so perfect: I had forgotten about the poster, and it was the first thing she noticed.

"Actually, that's my poster, I just put it up."

"The energy that moves the universe moves you. What does that mean?"

"That's ... well, that's what I was doing when I was meditating just now. It's a way to contact energy inside you. Here, have a seat." We both sat down at the kitchen table. "You have energy inside you, it's keeping you alive, and you can be aware of it through using your internal senses."

"What do you mean, internal senses?"

"It's a way to be aware of the energy inside you. You have a vibration inside you, and light, and sound, and a taste. And you can ... well, that's what the Knowledge is, that's what he means when he says, 'come and realize.' He shows a way to meditate on the energy inside. Which is what I was just doing."

She wanted to hear more, so I went on speaking. The words did not flow effortlessly out of me; after all, I had only been meditating about a month at that point, but she understood, and, I could tell she was hooked. She kept asking more and more questions, and we both got high sitting and talking about it.

Marie was seeking, she didn't know what, or why, but she was looking for something, a purpose beyond the various options life was offering. She was from Brazil, was at a crossroads, was not sure whether to go back home or not.

Then she broke down and started crying and admitted why she had come to my brother's apartment. She had been raped, and she'd been given this address because she'd been told there was a woman here who helped women in her situation.

Then she said, "But, I feel like I've found what I'm looking for. He's the reason I came here." She pointed at the poster. "To hear you talk about him. I don't think I need to talk to that woman now."

Before she left, we agreed to meet the next day to find the ashram in Minneapolis and attend satsang.

I was now doing what Guru Maharaj Ji had requested, telling others about the Knowledge, and it was exciting. I had felt such a rush from talking to her, and I was so glad I had followed that impulse to put up the poster.

When Ben came home, he was happy to see me, but clearly a little put-off by the poster on the refrigerator. I could see he was thinking, *What the fuck has happened to my kid brother?* He was only four years older than me but he had already graduated from college and been in the army. He had moved to Minneapolis after getting out of the army so he could do theater, which was his passion. We had really only known each other in the context of growing up in a large Catholic family. I had never hung out with him and his friends nor he with mine; there'd been too big an age difference.

I told him the story of the girl who'd come by, and he scratched his head and said, "I don't know anyone named Marie." For a moment he looked confused. "Oh, I know! She might have been looking for Sherry, my girl friend, you'll meet her, she stays here a lot. She has a friend at a clinic that supports abuse victims. Okay, yeah, that explains it."

The next day I found a job at a Japanese restaurant, which is where I worked for the next three weeks until I left for NYC. Marie and I went to the local ashram for satsang, and she loved it. A mahatma was scheduled to come through in a few weeks, and Marie became a regular at satsang; she eventually received the Knowledge.

When I was not working, I had nothing to do. Ben was busy with his new theater group and I didn't know anyone in Minneapolis, so I decided to check into other spiritual groups whose posters I saw around the city.

One Sunday I went to a spiritual gathering that looked interesting on the poster, but I discovered when I arrived that it was affiliated with Billy Graham and the Lutheran church. It had been a long bicycle ride getting there, so I stayed and I was surprised by the event; it almost reminded me of satsang with premies. Before the minister spoke, regular people from the congregation spoke in front of a microphone to the side of the stage. I could see them sitting by the side waiting their turn. Each person spoke for just a few minutes, but they had nothing prepared, they spoke without any notes, and it was from the heart and from their experience. Perhaps it was because I was so terrified of speaking in front of an audience that I was so impressed by people who, though clearly nervous, were able to get up there and speak like that. I felt something from listening to them which reminded me of what I felt listening to satsang. The only problem was that they often referenced the Bible, and the Christian terminology was a real turn-off.

Another group I checked into was called Eckankar. I had been intrigued by the posters I had seen of this group in Eugene, so when I saw a poster advertising a free intro program, I went. The presentation was like from a science fiction book. The man who spoke described soul travel, where the soul goes, and what the soul finds when it gets there. It was noteworthy to me that he *did* speak with notes. He was reading a presentation, and that was a red flag to me. Despite that, I found his description of planets, which represented different aspects of heaven, fascinating. For instance, on one planet the soul finds all the great saints who have ever lived, and these saints can be seen in their true aura colors and the sight is dazzling to the eyes. And the soul can travel to the astral plane, and can find out everything that has ever happened, and everything that ever will happen. The soul can travel through different levels of consciousness and the Eck is behind it all. The Eck is the energetic field from which everything comes.

It appealed to me very much. It reminded me of the chapter in *Autobiography of a Yogi* in which Yogananda receives a visit from his guru, who had recently died. His guru described to him this planet he was now on and his description was of paradise. However, as entertaining as it was, my bullshit detector sounded very loudly.

I interrupted the presentation at one point and asked, "Have you been to these planets you are describing?"

I did not intend to sound incredulous, but I realized he heard it that way. He said, "Please no questions until we are finished with the presentation."

After it was over I approached him and again asked him if he'd actually been to one of those places he had described.

"Our teacher, Paul Twitchell, has been and he shows us how to do it ourselves. Here, you can sign up here for the program."

The focus on getting a financial commitment was a real turn-off for me. As much as I really wanted it to be true, I knew there was no way I was going to pay money in the hopes that I could be taught how to do soul travel.

I could tell these followers of Eckankar had not actually been anywhere but were doing what they were doing in the hope that someday they would. I had no reason to doubt that their teacher had done the things he claimed and been to all those places he wrote about. After all, for the past year I had been visited a number of times by a presence that might very well be trying to tell me something, or take me somewhere, but I had been too terrified to take advantage of it.

One night I went to a meeting held by a group that was a part of the Gurdjieff Foundation. I was looking forward to this and went with the hope that I might learn something. I also had it in my head to to ask them about self-remembering. My own theory was that what I had been given by Guru Maharaj Ji, the meditation technique that could be done throughout the day, was really the key to self-remembering, and, if not the key, it certainly made it much more possible; that is, it quieted the voices in my head so I really could start to pay attention and self-remember. I wanted to ask someone about that who was actually involved with trying to self-remember. I remembered Jane's evasive answers to my questions and hoped that I would learn something practical at this meeting.

However, it proved to not be an interactive meeting. An older guy gave a lecture on states of being and levels of Man, all very theoretical. When he finished and asked for questions, I raised my hand, but when I started to ask my question about self-remembering he said I could only ask questions about what he had lectured about.

Afterwards, I tried to ask him my question, but he said that he would be giving a lecture on self-remembering in a few weeks and that it would be best if I came to that meeting so I could learn more about the subject. He had zero curiosity in me and what I had to say, so that was the end of that.

After being in Justin's meetings, this was a let down, and I realized I had no interest in whatever the Gurdjieff Foundation was doing, and that this confirmed in me the importance of a living teacher. Since Gurdjieff was long dead the group seemed to be stuck in a past age and whatever they were doing was not appropriate for the 1970s in America. It also confirmed for me that Justin's training must not have been with the Gurdjieff Foundation. I knew he was not officially with the group, but I thought maybe his style of conducting a meeting would be similar. It was not.

I also went to a Hare Krishna group for dinner, which made quite a strong impression on me. I really did feel like I was in some other century, or in some other place than modern day America. Everyone was dressed in orange robes chanting what they thought was the name of God. I knew about the Krishna people, but to be there in their midst was an other worldly, surreal experience. It reminded me so much of the Jesus house in Salt Lake City where everyone carried a bible and prayed to Jesus. The Krishna people carried copies of the Bhagavad Gita and did not pray but chanted the names of Krishna and Ram.

After dinner we were all guided into another room where the chanting was getting ready to begin. I tried talking to one of the guys in orange robes. I asked him what he thought of the possibility of the name of God being a vibration inside us, and not a sound made with the vocal chords. Nothing in what I said seemed to register in his eyes. He told me the name of God is Krishna and that it was so beautiful. He was so eager to start chanting it; I could see that he was on his path, to chant the name of Krishna, and he had no interest in discussing another possibility.

Okay, so why was I checking out all these other spiritual groups?

One part of me was incredulous that I had joined up so quickly with Guru Maharaj Ji. In checking out these other groups, I was looking for validation that I had either made a good choice, or that there was something out there just as good or better. In the various paths I looked into, I found nothing that attracted me. Guru Maharaj Ji's scene, as flawed as it was, came out looking pretty good.

The festival in London, called Guru Puja (Guru Worship), took place in two venues. We camped on land out in the suburbs, but the programs where Guru

Maharaj Ji would speak were in the city, so there was a lot of bus riding back and forth. The minimal amount of money I had paid allowed me to sleep in a large tent with many other people, and two meals a day, which proved to be a minimal amount of food, and I seemed to always be hungry. The weather was typical London weather, overcast, foggy, and never really warmed up until the final day.

By the time I arrived that first night, the outdoor program had already started, and I was directed by ushers to sit far in the back. I found it difficult to concentrate. The stage was crowded with people and was too far away for me to see who was speaking. I found out quickly that Guru Maharaj Ji was not on the stage because the person speaking was begging for him to come and give satsang. I was uncomfortable sitting on the ground, I was hungry, and I was jet lagged.

A woman named Suzy Bai was introduced to sing a song, and she started singing a song with a simple nursery rhyme-like melody:

> "Guru Maraji, you are so big,
> and I am so small,
> but when you smile, you shine for all,
> you shine for all, my Lord."

I had a strong negative reaction to her singing. I could not relate in any way to those words. I wondered why I was so small, and why was he so big? And what the hell does that mean anyway? Other than that I am worthless and insignificant and tell me something I don't already know, please!

This was my first immersion into the premie culture when Guru Maharaj Ji was close by, and his presence was a game changer. I was being put right up against my greatest obstacle in joining the premie group: devotion. I certainly resisted other aspects of the premie experience - the obsession with security, the diet of no meat, fish, or eggs, the Indian influence into the language - but none of those compared with my resistance to devotion.

Sitting cold and hungry on this land outside of London in this huge group of people listening to this woman singing a song of devotion to her Guru was *not* where I wanted to be. I did not have any desire or interest in being a devotee, and I did not want to end up like a babbling idiot singing a song of devotion to my guru, hoping he would come and allow me to see him.

I do think if my financial situation had been different I would have simply gotten up at that point and walked out. It was that bad. But I didn't have any money to stay somewhere for three days while I waited for my return flight home.

Why was I having such a strong disturbing reaction? It had been building up as I sat there and listened to the endless satsangs. The recurring theme was a call to Guru Maharaj Ji to come to the program. After all, we had traveled here from all over the world to see *him*, so, where was he?

With all the satsang begging Guru Maharaj Ji to come and appear in our midst, what happened to being here now? What happened to being aware in this present moment? The insistence that we really needed Guru Maharaj Ji struck me as weird and wrong. I thought the reason we had the Knowledge was so we could be connected inside.

According to the mahatmas giving satsang, Guru Maharaj Ji was not present because *we* were not ready. *We* were not calling out to him with the proper amount of love and devotion. It was our fault. It reminded me of my Catholic upbringing and all the *mea culpas* I had endured. It had been my fault that Jesus had to be crucified, and now it was my fault Guru Maharaj Ji was not coming to the program.

The inner dialogue in my head was in direct reaction to what was being said on stage. My inner dialogue was logical and correct, but I also knew that my logical and correct thinking had not done me much good in my life; it was something I wanted very much to get beyond.

I had to admit to myself, none of what was happening was a surprise. I knew enough about the premie culture to know the premie scene was all about devotion to the Guru. The name of the program, after all, was Guru Puja and puja means worship. As much as I might imagine or wish that it was about meditation and experiencing truth inside, I knew I had not come to London to close my eyes and meditate - I had come to London to open my eyes and see the Guru.

So,I had to ask myself, am I letting myself go into this experience, or am I holding on to how I have always been? Wasn't the point of coming here to try something new, to allow something new in, and then see what happened? I can always go back to how I was before. To be open to change requires being open to doing things differently, going against one's natural inclinations and predilections and behaviors.

Thus I reasoned with myself and talked myself into giving it another chance. And there was something else, too. I knew, deep down, far deeper down than I wanted to go, that the logical stream of my inner dialogue was bullshit. My problem was that I was afraid. I was terrified of devotion. I knew very well that the woman singing on stage was not faking it, she was connected to something inside and she was going with it. She was a devotee having the experience of devotion for her Guru and being exposed to that made me uncomfortable. This was all familiar territory to me, just like my negative reaction to Alonzo singing, "Amazing Grace."

I was still not where I needed to be. I still had not done what I knew I had to do. I was still holding on to my critical thoughts about all of this. I had come thousands of miles to see Guru Maharaj Ji, but

I was still unwilling to let myself go and sing a simple song to him with the hope that he would come on stage. And he never did come that night. Probably because of me.

Just kidding!

The next morning after the group meditation I showed up at the breakfast serving area determined to make a fresh start. Two people brought out a huge pot from a tent and set it down. One of them pointed to me and said, "You want to do some service?"

"Sure," I said.

He handed me the ladle and said, "Don't give out too big a portion." Then he demonstrated, showing me how much to put into a bowl. I didn't say anything, but I was thinking, "That's a very small portion." He looked at me and said, "I know what you're thinking, it's small, but we have a lot of people who need to eat, and we don't want to run out." Then he leaned in and said confidentially, "And there's some put aside for us, you'll get a nice big bowl-full when we're done."

With the promise of getting more than everyone else, I stepped behind the huge, steaming pot of mush. When the premies came by holding out their bowls, I ladled a portion into it. Most of the premies were coming from the group meditation and were wrapped up in blankets or colorful sheets, and I had a beautiful time, looking into each person's face as they approached holding their bowl out to me, and I tried not to look at their disappointed expression after I gave them their meager portion.

The feeling of being connected to humanity caught me off guard; it was not something I had been looking for on this trip, and I have to say that it was a big reason London was such a positive experience for me. The gray overcast day out on this piece of land could have been anywhere in the world and at any time in history. I had a sense of taking part in a timeless drama that has been reenacted all over the world, in so many different cultures when devotees gather together to see their Master. As different as we all were, we shared this common desire, to find God within and to be in our Master's physical presence. As weird and out of it as I had felt the night before, I now felt the opposite. A good night's sleep and meditation had given me a beautiful feeling of being connected to everyone I saw. Many different nationalities were represented on the campsite. A large percentage were from India, but also, many blonde Northern Europeans, dark-haired southern Europeans, Asians, Latino premies from South America, all different shades of humanity were represented and in each person's eyes I saw the same thing, the light of life and consciousness. I did not see a certain nationality looking out at me, but I saw inside those eyes a presence, someone just like me, connected to the same thing I was connected to within.

A girl in line started singing the song, "We are one in the spirit, we are one in the Lord." Before my mind could tell me how much I did not like that song, I opened my mouth and joined in along with others in the line. I was feeling the words I was singing. It was a beautiful moment because it was expressing what we were all feeling, that we are one with each other. We are all the same, it is the grand illusion that we are different from each other.

At one point someone rushed up and shouted, "Maharaji's here, he's driving around the camp!"

He then ran away. There was a moment of confusion as people looked around. What to do? Some premies left the line and started running. I felt a jolt of excitement in my stomach, and I did not know what I was supposed to do. My hands gripped the serving ladle a little tighter. I was glad I had a job to do so I could easily rationalize not running around looking like an idiot.

Someone said, "Where are people rushing off to? If he's driving around the campsite, he might drive right by here."

That certainly made sense, and the moment of anxiety subsided, the line resumed with people keeping their eyes and ears open.

However sensible it sounded, it also sounded like a cop-out, rationalizing the reluctance to look foolish. There was something childlike and natural about dropping everything and running. Silly? Sure! But to whom exactly? And who wants to be serious about this anyway?

You can look for it, but it will do you no good even if you can find a book describing the proper behavior for a devotee to the Guru. In that relationship, anything goes, and that makes it scary. I could not look at anyone else and know what to do. I was on my own, it was just me and the Guru.

That night's program was in a large hall in London, and Guru Maharaj Ji's talk was to be geared for the general public; so, first, we had a parade that would let everyone know about the program. We assembled in downtown London and then marched to Trafalgar Square handing out leaflets along the way, inviting people to come to the program that night. During this parade I had another bout of feeling separate and weird. I wasn't at a level of experience where I could engage strangers in conversation about the Knowledge, and the parade struck me as ... well, just completely strange. For instance, there were huge signs proclaiming that Guru Maharaj Ji was the Lord of the Universe. I dropped out after a few blocks and enjoyed exploring London, a city I had never visited before.

That evening I went to the Hall for the program. The Hall had a large stage at one end, rows of folding chairs set up for the audience, and then at the back an exhibit designed to educate the masses about the concept and history of Perfect Masters. I walked through the exhibit looking at the pictures of past Masters and reading the descriptions of their lives. All the famous ones who had started religions were represented: Jesus, Buddha, Mohammed, Ram, Krishna. And there were many I had never heard of before. I was surprised see the Hasidic saint, the Baal Shem Tov, "Master of the Divine Name" represented. He was the one in that book David had loaned me. It was strange to imagine that now I had the same secret knowledge those Hasidic masters had, and I laughed imagining what David would say about all this.

And yes, I did certainly question if it even was the secret knowledge. I mean, how could I have been so lucky? How could it all have happened so easily for me? Yet, I could not argue or reason away the experience I had in meditation of the cessation of my inner dialogue. That was not something I could doubt, and I knew that was not a product of my imagination. Also, since I had started meditating, I had been sleeping at night like a baby. I'd had no trouble falling asleep. The voices in my head no longer kept me awake, and they had been keeping me awake since I'd been in high school. Whether it was the same secret knowledge that Masters in the past had also revealed was irrelevant to me - whatever it was, it worked.

However, I was still not a happy camper. The problem? The stage. It was a ridiculously high stage and there were five thrones on it! If the point of all this was to give this Knowledge to the general public, I had to wonder what will the general public think of the five thrones on the stage?

I was getting into my mind again, a premie term, probably the most used premie term of all at that time. I think this is as good a time as any to try and explain it.

Tom Wolfe wrote a book called the *Electric Kool-Aid Acid Test,* which described the escapades of

Ken Kesey and his band of Merry Pranksters. In the mid 60s they took LSD and drove all over the country in an old school bus, driving into small towns and making a scene out of it by dropping acid and hanging out there. *On the bus* was an expression they used to describe their ability to go with the flow of what was happening. If you were *on the bus*, that meant you were cool, you were with it, you were in the flow of the moment, you were digging life. If you were *off the bus*, you were uptight, feeling weird, out of it, or feeling paranoid, or pissed off about something - basically, not feeling connected to what was happening in the moment. This expression was used, over-used, and eventually corrupted by me and my friends to describe how we felt about any given situation.

Premies used the expression *in my mind* to describe the *off the bus* feeling. If I was *in my mind*, then I was stuck in my head, thinking too much, worried, feeling separate, doubting. If I was not in my mind, then I was feeling connected via the flow of the Knowledge within. So, I'd been *on the bus* during the morning, serving food to the premies, and now at the program looking at the stage I was most definitely *off the bus, in my mind*.

I sat down somewhere in the middle of the auditorium and waited for the festivities to begin, wondering how to get myself back on the bus, but staring at the stage was not helping. It went up and up and up. There were five thrones arranged in a pyramid, and at the top was Guru Maharaj Ji's. At each throne were many, many flowers with the most flowers surrounding the top throne. Premies kept coming out and adjusting or changing something on or around the thrones. And each time they did, they bowed down to the empty thrones. I felt like I was about to have an audience with the Wizard of Oz.

The five thrones represented a big problem for me. I could understand one throne, but why did the three brothers and the mother also need thrones? They called themselves the Holy Family, but what did the word *holy* mean, anyway? Were they also, all of them, saints? And were we supposed to bow down to all of them? Did we have to bow a deeper and more reverent bow to Guru Maharaj Ji? Again, I had an attack of wanting to run, but knew I would stay for the program. I had not yet seen Guru Maharaj Ji, so I was looking forward to seeing him and hearing him speak.

When the music started, that certainly helped to change my mood. The second oldest of Guru Maharaj Ji's brothers, Bhole Ji, was a musician. He was referred to as the god of music reincarnated into Guru Maharaj Ji's family to help spread the Knowledge to the world. It was one of those facts thrown around by premies that I successfully ignored, meaning I did not take it seriously, and I also did not let it bother me. Bhole Ji seemed to be a pretty cool guy. He was dressed in a sharp looking suit and looked very serious as he conducted Blue Aquarius, the name of his twenty-five piece orchestra. There were horns and strings, but it also had electric guitars, and they mainly played rock music. They started with a bang, playing a very cool version of "Purple Haze," the Jimi Hendrix hit. I was on my feet with most of the premies, moving to the beat.

After the band played, a few mahatmas spoke, and then Guru Maharaj Ji's oldest brother, Bal Bagwhan Ji spoke. He was supposedly the "intellectual" of the family, representing the god of mathematics and science. And I did enjoy hearing him speak. He must have been about 21, so he was about my age, and I certainly had to admit I could never do what he was doing.

Eventually, and with much fanfare, Guru Maharaj Ji came out on stage. I duly noted that I didn't feel anything special. I did enjoy hearing him speak though. His voice and manner of speaking were unassuming and non-authoritative, and I listened intently, enjoying the flow of his talk. He spoke in a fairly simple English - I think he had only completed 9th grade at this point - but I could understand most of what he said.

He told a story that I heard him tell more than once, which I will repeat here.

> *A rich man died and went up to heaven and knocked on the pearly gates, and St. Peter came to the door and wanted to know what this man had done to make him he think he should be in heaven.*
>
> *The man thought and thought and then he said, "Oh, I know! Once I gave two cents to a beggar on the street."*
>
> *St. Peter nodded his head and said, "Okay, well, anything else?"*
>
> *The man thought some more and said, "Oh yeah, once I gave three cents to a blind man."*
>
> *St. Peter heard this and looked at him as if to say, anything else? The man thought and thought but could not think of anything else.*
>
> *So, St. Peter is not sure what to do. The man had done some good in his life, so maybe he should get into heaven. At that moment God happened to*

be walking by, and St. Peter said, "Oh, hi God, I'm glad you showed up just now. This is an interesting situation. We have this man and he has done some good in his life, but I'm not sure it's enough. He gave two cents to a beggar once and also, three cents to a blind man."

So God looked at the man, and then he said to St. Peter, "Give him his nickel back and tell him to go to hell."

The message? That heaven, being in heaven, is not a product of good deeds. It does not matter how much good you do in your life, if you do not have the inner connection, you cannot experience God.

The next and final day, darshan was scheduled. Darshan was what they called bowing down before Guru Maharaj Ji and kissing his feet. Since I had not done it before, I wondered exactly how it would all work. Premies described it to me, but I had trouble picturing it in my mind. My main concern was what exactly would be expected of me? When would I bow down, how long I would have in front of him, would I have a chance to speak to him? I knew I was supposed to kiss his feet, but I didn't really want to kiss his feet. Would I have to? Or could I just bow down?

I wanted to give myself plenty of time to prepare, so by the time I joined the line, it was very long, winding all around the campsite, and that was fine with me - I was in no hurry. We stood there for some time before the line even started to move, and there was little conversation happening. The people I was standing next to had no interest in talking to me, and I had no interest in talking to them. Who knows, maybe what was going on in my head was happening in their heads, too.

It was an overcast day but not raining and it was warmer than it had been, so I was not uncomfortable standing there, and yet for a certain part of me, it was torturous. That part of me was not happy at all to be standing in a line waiting to kiss the feet of a guru. And yet, I knew I had to do it, I had to check this out all the way.

I knew the only reason I did not want to do it was that I was afraid. But what was I afraid of? Why was I afraid to bow down before this teenager from India? Because it was an unknown experience, outside of my control. My objecting part had no concrete reason to offer for *not* doing it, other than, it was afraid. The only thing holding me back was fear. Fear of becoming a devotee is what it boiled down to. I was afraid to become a devotee. I was afraid of becoming *that* vulnerable, *that* out of control, *that* *emotional.* I flashed back on how I had seen Justin behaving at that program when he was weeping like a baby in the aisle. Nothing was more terrifying to me than becoming like that. *That* I knew was beyond me.

Fortunately, I was able to focus on the internal meditation technique and allow myself to just be there, to just stand in line and move with it as it slowly moved. At the previous night's program I had been more off the bus than on it, but now I was simply there, letting the impressions wash over me, and not feeling much in the way of separation or connection. I had no expectations for the experience I was about to go through. I had no wish or interest in trying to imagine what would happen, I just wanted to follow through on that decision I had made in Eugene. I would bow down before the person who claimed to be the source of this newfound inner connection.

At some point we were instructed to have an offering, something to give when we came to Guru Maharaj Ji. Many of us had picked one of the many small wildflowers growing all around and held them, which became perhaps my strongest memory of that day, standing silently in a line with strangers, on a gray warm day, holding a tiny flower.

After several hours of moving slowly along, I came close enough to where I could see Guru Maharaj Ji. He was sitting in a chair surrounded by many premies and everyone looked very busy. He seemed to be deep in conversation with one of them, while premies were constantly flowing before him, moved along by a line of people before and after him. And he did not seem to be paying attention to them at all. People were being pushed along, pushed along, then pushed down, then being pulled away, pushed away, and then let go. Terror gripped me. It looked so bizarre. On the other side of where the guru sat, people were falling down, crying out, shouting, laughing; many just scurried off, and many immediately sat down, closed their eyes, and meditated.

The line drew ever nearer, and the air began to buzz. The sweetest, most intoxicating smell filled the air, which I learned later was the smell of gardenias, a flower that I was not familiar with. In this fast approaching situation, I had no idea what I was supposed to be, but fortunately I didn't have to do anything. It was all done to me. Twenty feet away I was being passed from one person to the next. I could hear him laughing and talking to someone in his high, energetic voice. He was animated, pointing at someone, shouting out to someone behind him. I was pushed down in front of him and then dragged up and handed off to other people who were on the other side of the line, helping people to navigate their way to an open part of the field. Then I was sitting down, joining others who were just staring at the scene. I closed my eyes and didn't have to meditate. I felt the flow of the energy inside. Then I'd remember I could be looking at Guru Maharaj Ji, so I'd open my eyes and stare at him and get fascinated and distracted by a scene I could not figure out. Guru Maharaj Ji was so active. I thought I did not have any expectations, but I must have, because what I saw surprised me. I was expecting the guru to be sitting still and receiving his followers and that it would be a contemplative, quiet, serene scene. I was to learn from future experiences he had no set way of behaving, but when I first saw him doing this, he never stopped talking, laughing, gesturing, paying a great deal of attention to everything happening all around him.

I couldn't deny the buzzy feeling that I had felt which seemed to be in the air surrounding him. But how much of that weird buzz was manufactured by the strange physical circumstances? All those people pushing me and pulling me along, how much did that have to do with my experience? I certainly had not felt any personal connection with him, he was not looking at me when I went by, and I hardly had time to glance at him, so I did not get to look at him directly in the eyes. I thought it ironic that the first time I bowed down to my guru, I didn't do the bowing down; I was pushed down and brought back up again.

So, I was neither convinced nor unconvinced. I did have the thought that I wished I could do it again, that I had not really done it right, it had happened too quickly. There was something appealing to me about bowing down.

After the darshan line ended, the sky cleared up and the sun came out, and people started to congregate in small groups around the site. In one such group a mahatma was speaking to a small group of premies and I joined them. I learned later his name was Rajeswar. He seemed to be well-educated and knew English better than most of the mahatmas. He was also dressed in different clothes than the orange-robed mahatmas with shaved heads. He had a normal head of hair and was dressed in dark Indian clothes. A premie asked him a question about drugs, specifically about an LSD trip he had taken in which he had seen a white light. He wondered what drug experiences had to do with the Knowledge. Was it the same light?

Rajeswar said, "Guru Maharaji sent LSD to the west to prepare all of you for Knowledge. Yes, of course it's the same light! There is only one light! There is not one light over here and another light over there, there is only one light and LSD can show you this light, and that is why I say, LSD was sent to you to get you ready, to open your mind to the possibility of this inner experience. LSD can take you there, but you cannot *stay* there by LSD. Only through the Knowledge can you have it for yourself always."

When he said that Guru Maharaj Ji had sent LSD to the west to prepare us for Knowledge, I took that as a joke, it sounded so outrageous, but after thinking about it I realized there was certainly truth to the idea that LSD had prepared me for Knowledge. After all, why did the Knowledge and this inner experience make so much sense to me?

My Catholic upbringing had not mentioned to me that an *experience* was at the root of religion and spirituality - just the opposite, in fact. Faith was considered the root of it all. So why did the Knowledge, with its promise of an inner experience, make so much sense to me? The answer is LSD. LSD had given me an inner experience that, for me, had been an experience of being in touch with something higher, a higher emotion, a higher feeling, a connection to something greater than me: love, not for a pretty girl, but love for every living thing. I know that not everyone who took LSD had a spiritual experience, but I certainly did. So in that sense, LSD did prepare me for the idea of spirituality being an experience.

But it was not the only thing that prepared me. In support of that experience, Jesus does say in the Bible, "The kingdom of heaven is within." I did not see what else that could mean other than that heaven was an experience within my mind and consciousness.

Later, at the final evening's program in London, I was determined to not follow my usual way of doing things. I would not fall victim to my own negative thinking, I was gonna get out of my mind, my head, my habitual behavior, and get myself on the bus! I pushed my way through to get as close to the front as possible and found myself sitting on the floor fairly close to the stage surrounded by premies who were feeling no pain. Maybe it was the darshan experience that had loosened me up, but I was able to just let down my guard and have fun. Someone started singing a devotional song, and I joined in loudly. We were not stuck in an attitude of waiting for something to happen, we were making it happen, sitting cross-legged on the floor with our arms around each other, rocking back and forth. We continued to sing songs until Bhole Ji came out and the band started playing hits from the 60s. And that immediately got us all on our feet dancing.

When Guru Maharaj Ji spoke, I did not feel anything special. This was the second time he had spoken, and he made the point that peace is within, and feeling good, feeling peace, has nothing to do with externals. At that time there was a lot of publicity about Guru Maharaj Ji and his fancy cars and his money. Since he didn't charge for the Knowledge, and the programs were free, I didn't understand the criticism, but he did talk about that and he made the point that he was the richest man in the world because he was rich in heart. And he also spoke about the terrible condition of the world and that his purpose in leaving India and coming to the west was to spread this knowledge so everyone in the world could have the chance to experience it. This certainly resonated with me. The world was fucked up in a major way, and if I had been helped so quickly by the Knowledge, maybe others could also be helped.

The most important thing was that I felt good when the program ended. I was happy; I was on the bus. Nothing dramatic had happened, I had not seen a flash of brilliant white light, and I had not felt anything definitive during darshan; still, I knew that this simple beautiful feeling inside me when the program ended was the confirmation I'd been looking for. I liked being around premies. I liked the idea of helping to spread the Knowledge, and I liked the focus on what was happening inside, the focus on paying attention inside. I knew I would go against all those objecting voices in my head. I would go back to America and join in full time. I would become a premie to help Guru Maharaj Ji spread the Knowledge.

But that is another story.

THE END

Comments?
You may contact the author at this email address:
kampey@gmail.com

Made in the USA
Charleston, SC
06 July 2016